Timur's Escape

TABI SLICK

Copyright © 2019 by Tabi Slick
Cover art copyright © 2019 SWC Indie Press

This is a work of historical fiction. Names, characters, places, events, and incidents are either products of the author's imagination or are used fictitiously. Where real-life figures appear, the situations, incidents, and dialogues concerning those persons are entirely fictional and are not intended to change the entirely fictional nature of the work. In all other respects, any resemblance to persons living or dead is entirely coincidental.

All rights reserved. No part of this book may be reproduced, or stored in a retrieval system, or transmitted in any form or by any means, electronic, mechanical, photocopying, recording, or otherwise, without express written permission of the author.

Published by SWC Indie Press
www.SWCindiepress.com

Second Edition, 2019.

ISBN: 978-1727433746 (First Edition)
ISBN: 978-0-578-43310-3 (Paperback)
ISBN: 978-0-578-43822-1 (Ebook)

Printed in the United States of America

Edited by Sarah Burton:
AnAvidReader.com

Visit the author's website at www.TabiSlick.com

Contents

Dedication	6
Historical Note	8
Prologue	13
CHAPTER 1: Friday Selamlık	18
CHAPTER 2: Görücülük	28
CHAPTER 3: Divan-ı Hümâyûn	43
CHAPTER 4: The Köçek	55
CHAPTER 5: Don't Fear the Ubir	66
CHAPTER 6: Confusion at the Palace	79
CHAPTER 7: Söz Kesimi	90
CHAPTER 8: The Conspiracy	101
CHAPTER 9: A Body in the Water	115
CHAPTER 10: Dead Man	128
CHAPTER 11: The Danger in Hope	139
CHAPTER 12: Betrayal	151
CHAPTER 13: Kına Gecesi	163
CHAPTER 14: Treason	173
CHAPTER 15: Gelin Alma	185
Epilogue	199
More Transitioned Universe Books	203

Glossary	205
Bibliography	211
Acknowledgements	214
About the Author	215
Connect with the Author	217

Dedication

To my loving husband,

you're an endless source of inspiration.

Historical Note

The Ottoman Empire has long been an intriguing mystery to me. Being not only the largest empire, but also the longest empire in human history, it was curious that my World History class in High School only touched on the subject for no more than a single chapter. Over a decade later, give or take a few years, I decided to finally settle into researching this faraway place. All of my books are connected by time and so I knew my next novel would have to be written in the 17th century. Focusing on this time period of the Ottoman Empire still required research of the past, but it allowed me to focus more on just a few hundred years rather than the entire six-hundred years of the Ottoman Empire.

There are a few alternative events that happen in Timur's Escape and I feel it important to understand what really happened before diving into this entirely fictional story. The story is based on a few alternate events that takes place during the reign of Sultan Mustafa II, who ruled from 1695 to 1703. Historically, Mustafa II's father, Mehmed IV, died when Mustafa II was in his late twenties and of natural causes. Mustafa II did not succeed after his father's death, however. Mustafa II's uncle, Suleiman II, took the throne, if you will, from 1687 until his death in 1691. But still, Mustafa II did not become sultan. The title went to his other uncle, Ahmed II, until he also died just four years later. Both of Mustafa II's uncles died at the Edirne Palace. Mustafa II finally became the sultan, but we can't forget his mother's hand in the matter.

Mustafa II was the son of Mehmed IV's chief escort, Emetullah Rabia Gülnuş. One of the lead female characters, Queen Naz, is based on this remarkable woman for a number of reasons. She was a captive to the Ottomans and sent to the Topkapı Palace as a concubine. There she received an extensive education and quickly became Sultan Mehmed IV's favorite. They had two sons, Mustafa II and Ahmed III. But her position was soon threatened by another woman in the harem. Emetullah was known to be very jealous and so it is said that she had the other woman killed. It's unclear whether or not she drowned the other woman or had her strangled, but she had a hand in removing the opposing woman to ensure her son became the sultan. It was important for the chief escort to birth a son because it would likely be their son who would receive the title of sultan one day, thus promoting the chief escort to valide sultan. Valide sultan was the most influential position a woman could have in the Ottoman Empire. It is also rumored that Emetullah made several attempts to have Sultan Mehmed IV's brothers, Suleiman II and Ahmed II, murdered. Once Mustafa II became sultan, his mother took position of valide sultan and became a powerful political leader. Mustafa II was known to be very attached to his mother and would not only consult her on state affairs, but would often have her accompany him to meetings. She intervened in many political situations and had a reputation of being a cunning leader.

My years of research have not only revealed a long history within the Ottoman Empire of deposing its sultans, but it has also unveiled a history of vampiric occurrences. The vampires of Timur's Escape are fundamentally based on the Turkish mythology of vampires known as "Ubir". I never imagined that my research would lead me to discover real-life vampires. There are legal transcripts dated as early as the 15th century documenting Turkish villagers complaining to the supreme judge about how the recently deceased would return to their homes at night asking the villagers to go out with them. Those who went would be found dead in the morning, drained of blood. The problem continued even into the 16th and 17th centuries where it's reported by the Turkish explorer, Evliya Çelebi, that there were professional Ubir hunters. Many of Evliya Çelebi's written sightings of vampires have been said to resemble Bram Stoker's "Dracula", written over a hundred years later.

Timur's Escape is inspired by a respectful marriage between history and folklore, of culture and passion, and a tale filled with love. It's not just about the vampires and the inner workings of the Ottoman Empire, but also about the way of life, the delicious food, and the architecture of the time. It is a fictional story where one can learn about life as a Turk in a 17th century Ottoman Empire.

Prologue

Ottoman Empire, mid-17th century.

A peculiar silence filled the streets of Constantinople, one that would leave the bravest soldier trembling in fear. Not a soul could be seen, save for a shadow that lurked beneath a window of the Imperial Harem. The figure's dark cloak fluttered in the night's breeze as she scaled the stone walls. Upon slipping through the opening, the intruder swept past the many rooms belonging to the sultan's wives, concubines, and eunuchs with a speed unknown to man. After the hundredth pillar, she stopped.

The shadow reached for the door and slipped into the chamber, her footsteps no louder than a moth fluttering in the wind. Moonlight illuminated a spacious room blanketed with rare carpets and sofas. At its center, a large canopy made of India's finest silks hung above the bed cushion where a woman laid, fast asleep. A sudden movement halted the intruder's advances. From behind the woman, a little boy sat up, blinking owlishly back at the intruder.

"Be still, Mustafa," her soothing voice whispered from underneath the cloak.

With one swift movement, she removed the hood. Naz's cunning eyes sparkled bronze in the moonlight that illuminated the room. Her ivory skin glowed against onyx hair that fell in neat waves. For a moment her pupils dilated and her hazel irises were replaced with fire. The sultan's only son and heir stood before her, tears streaming down his face. A cry escaped him, threatening to wake the sleeping woman. She swiftly stepped forward, securing her gaze on the child.

"You are not in danger," her melodic voice whispered.

The power in her words curled through the air and landed on Mustafa. He became mesmerized, his eyes frozen on hers. With a wave of her hand, the child obediently moved from the bed and backed himself into the farthest corner of the chamber. Satisfied that the child would not be in her way, she crept closer to the woman that lay on the bed. She lowered herself inches from the sleeping woman's enchanting face, taking in her scent. Bringing her hand to the woman's neck, she caressed her pulsating vein before plunging her teeth into its depths. She sighed with satisfaction as the metallic taste of the woman's blood hit her parted lips. Growing stronger with each swallow, the woman's life force filled her.

When she had thoroughly depleted the woman, she looked up at the child. He acted as if he were trying to speak, but that wasn't possible. He was under her control and would speak when it was finished. When her plan was complete.

"Hush, my little one," she cooed.

In one swift movement, she leaped from the bed to kneel next to him, resting her blood-drenched hands on his shoulders.

"There, there," she whispered, wiping away the boy's tears. "It will be okay. The monster's gone."

Pupils pulsating, she locked her gaze onto the child's, infiltrating his mind with her own. The memory of the last few minutes hung in his mind and she carefully pulled at it, forming a new one with her as his mother.

"Mommy has killed the bad lady." Naz rose, stretching her hand out. "Come, you can rest easy now."

The boy took her hand and she smiled triumphantly. Everything was going according to plan. It was time to make sure the rest did as well. Turning to leave, she nearly ran into a beast of a man. His dark skin contrasted against the white silk robe and turban he donned.

"Is it done, Bayar?" She asked the Imperial Harem's kizlar chief. "Have they taken care of the sultan?"

"Yes, my queen," he replied, giving a single nod. His smooth, young face glowing in the night. Even though he was well in age, he didn't look a day older than when she found him.

"Good." Her eyes sparkled with delight, satisfied by the news.

It would only be a matter of time before the son of the late Sultan Mehmed's chief consort inherited the empire. She eyed her other warriors as they cleaned the room of the body, leaving no traces behind. A delighted chuckled escaped her lips, realizing how close she was to assuming the title of valide sultan and all the power that came with it.

"What's happening, Mama?"

"Nothing, my sweet one," Queen Naz replied as a victorious smile grew upon her lips.

The child believed that she was his mother even after she had killed her right in front of him. How much easier would it be to compel a few strangers that she was the chief consort and next in line to become valide sultan? Without the sultan alive to confirm, it would be her word against any challenger.

Bayar cleared his throat, his feet shifting nervously in the presence of the queen.

"Is there something else?" She asked, her voice etched with impatience.

"It's your son," he began.

"My son?" She asked, looking down at her newly acquired child.

"Your *true* son."

Her eyes flashed amber, warning him to watch his tongue. "I gave you a new life," she hissed, "A purpose when you were mutilated and alone and I can just as easily take it all away. I have only one son that matters now."

Bayar quickly nodded, acknowledging he understood before leaving the chamber. They had much work to do to secure her position as valide sultan. She could no longer worry about her biological child.

CHAPTER 1: Friday Selamlık

Many years later.

Spiced helva, coffee and freshly-baked simit perfumed the bezesten as Emel's younger sister pulled her towards the exit. She was sad she couldn't stay to enjoy more of the bustling marketplace, but Sidika was determined to leave.

"I don't know why we have to go already," Emel said, her voice etched with disappointment.

True, she had all but dragged Sidika out of the house to go exploring. If the shoe was on the other foot she would be thanking her older sister, not scolding her.

"We're not even supposed to be out of the house," Sidika whispered, adjusting her yasmak for the hundredth time. "Especially not without a chaperone."

"Who says?" The glare Emel received to her question was her only answer.

"If we're not home soon, Mama will notice. Or worse." Sidika was uneasy, jumping at each merchant's holler or abrupt scuttle of a cart passing by. Emel felt sorry for her. Sidika didn't deserve a life of fear, but her sister couldn't argue that it was one of her own making. Sidika chose to believe in all of the nonsense the maids gossiped about. From the strange herb that Manula called tutku flower—she would sneak into their tea—to insisting they get out of bed on the right side instead of the left no matter how inconvenient.

"What has you scared now?" Emel stopped to admire a cart piled high with rugs she imagined were from faraway places. Exotic regions she hoped to one day see.

The delicate texture tickled her fingertips, reminding her of the pink silk tree blossoms that framed their house.

"Manula says she heard an Ubir was spotted on this very street."

"What?" She scoffed. "Manula makes things up. I promise you, even if the Ubir were real they wouldn't be spotted in broad daylight."

Emel couldn't remember a time when their maid wasn't going on about how the Ubir were a true threat to Constantinople. Sure, she remembered hearing the stories of beasts that roamed the night for food. Powerful beings that craved what was unfit for a human body. They preyed greedily on the blood of women and children. Yet, these were mere bedtime stories used to scare children and girls from leaving the confines of their home.

"But if the Ubir did exist I'd rather like to meet one, wouldn't you?" Emel asked her sister.

"What? Absolutely not!" Sidika retorted. "How could you say such a thing?"

"I'd have a lot of questions, like how do they find food, what type of abilities do they have, that sort of thing."

A pale complexion flooded Sidika's cheeks as if Emel's words were making her ill.

"Come on, Sidika." She urged her sister to test out the rug the Frank was offering. "You need to learn to live a little."

Her sister made no effort to feel the fabric.

"Please?" She asked, batting her eyelashes.

"Fine." She sighed, yanking the rug from Emel, the force of it pulling the yasmak off of Emel's face.

Sidika shrieked, startling the Frank beside them as she quickly pulled Emel out of his sight.

"I'm so sorry! Let me help you before anyone sees you." Sidika's hands shook as she attempted to fix Emel's indecency.

"So what?" She asked, not caring for her sister's prudence, "What could anyone do?"

"You know what could happen," Sidika replied, a warning look flooding her mahogany eyes. "What if the traders saw you, your golden brown hair, your uniqueness and took you?"

"It's fine, okay?" With her face fully covered now, Emel swatted her sister's prodding hands away. "Everything is going to be fine. No one saw."

"You don't know that." Sidika shook fearfully.

"Sidika." The authority in her voice clear. "I'm your older sister. I'm asking you for once to please stop worrying. Besides, it's nearing midday so we should be getting back. Just like you wanted, okay?"

"Thank you." Sidika's shoulders relaxed as relief washed over her.

Placing the bezesten behind them, they made their way through the throngs of people. It never ceased to amaze Emel how many Franks from all over the world filled the streets. The abrupt shouts of the Armenian carpenters and Jewish merchants clashed with the graceful Persian voices that all floated through the air like music to her ears.

"Are you looking forward to your meeting?" Sidika asked, pulling Emel from her musings.

She cringed, having just turned the suitable age for marriage, a number of women with sons had been approaching her mother in the hopes of making an arrangement. She already had an astonishing number of prospects. After dressing in her finest, their mother, Funda, would parade her around in front of the prospective mother-in-law like a prized lamb to be slaughtered.

"How could I possibly look forward to such a thing?" She replied, swatting at a buzzing mosquito.

The attempt was futile as the humidity in the air provided a perfect climate for them.

"You don't want to be married?" Sidika scoffed, "But there is no honor in life—"

"For a woman unmarried. Yes, I know what mother says and I do want to be married. But I don't want an arrangement."

"But there's no other way."

"What if we could choose?"

Sidika remained silent as they continued their trek. The buildings became less dense as they neared the outskirts of the city. The delicious scent of the ocean became more distinct as they neared their home. Turning the corner, they were nearly trampled by a group of gruff looking leventis who must've just arrived back from sea. The smell of putrid fish and dried cypress lingered as they ducked past them.

"What if you could marry for love or desire?" Passion filled Emel's soul as she continued. "What if you found a man you could converse with as an equal, so edifying you couldn't imagine a life without him?"

Taking a deep breath, she continued to fantasize about what it would be like to marry whomever she wished as she waited for her sister's scolding. She imagined it would be much like the freedom of swimming in the ocean. Running down the bank without a care in the world as the gritty sand squished between her toes. To feel the silky water wrapped around her body. It was as much a forbidden pleasure to the daughter of a nishanji as it was for a woman to choose her own groom. Their father, Hasan-Ali, was the nishanji of the Imperial Council and it was more likely she would be married off to a diplomat than it was for her to marry of her own choosing.

"That isn't the way," Sidika replied. "And who's to say the feelings would last? A flame burns bright at first, but then quickly runs out. Then you're left with a man who can't even provide a daily cup of coffee."

They continued down the cobblestone path in silence, Emel having no words for her little sister. Partly because deep in her heart she did not want Sidika to be right. They were always told what to think, say, and do. Emel was determined that love would be the one thing that was hers to find for herself. Despite what her family and society said, she knew there was a lasting love for her. There had to be.

"The sultan is coming!" a little boy exclaimed, interrupting her thoughts as he ran past.

The boy was quickly berated by his father, pulling him out of the way. A loud horn echoed between the adobe and wooden homes that framed the street. People pushed their way to the sidewalk to make room, shoving Emel and her sister to the furthest corner. They ducked behind a group of Turkish women, their white head-coverings providing the perfect coverage as they peered through the crowd at the approaching parade.

"We're going to get in trouble for this." Sidika groaned.

"Shh," Emel warned as the pages marched on foot, guiding the steed that carried Sultan Mustafa.

The presence of the sultan swept across the crowd, who stood in awe of the precession taking place. It was Emel's first time to see the sultan parade through town. On the rare occasion she managed to escape the house it had always been at the wrong time. Her heart leaped as the solaks came into view, their pointed hats with a line of large feathers affixed to the top making them impossible not to notice. They were the sultan's personal guards.

"Come, I want to get a closer look." She motioned for Sidika to follow her.

"What? Are you crazy?"

Emel glanced back, her sister crossing her arms in defiance. She was determined to stand in the back.

Emel shrugged. "Suit yourself."

Ducking and elbowing her way through the crowd, she made it to the front just in time to see the sultan nearly face-to-face. The sun glistened down upon him, his neatly groomed beard matching the reddish hue of the steed he rode. His facial hair covered most of his expression, but his eyes surprised her. They were cloudy, vacant of life. A shiver ran down her spine as he looked straight through her.

Is this how he normally looks? She wondered.

Distracted by the sultan, her foot caught on a rock catapulting her into the street. Her body pitched towards the ground and she squeezed her eyes shut, anticipating the pain that was soon to follow.

A strong arm wrapped around her waist and her fall was halted. With a hammering heart, she opened her eyes. The road a mere inch away from her nose. She couldn't believe she hadn't it the ground. It was impossible to catch anyone at that speed.

"Are you alright?" A rich and deep voice melted in her ear.

She was pulled to her feet, allowing her to see the sorrel-brown eyes of the one who saved her. His dark eyebrows furrowed and she instinctively reached for her yasmak. Satisfied that her face was still covered, she wondered why he was staring. Their eyes locked and for a moment she was lost in his gaze. His expression seemed gentle, yet guarded, and for a moment his irises flickered crimson so quickly she almost thought she'd imagined it.

The whisper of arrows being drawn pulled her from her trance. She was surrounded by the rest of the solak guard, their aim ready to fire at her. She glanced up at the solak who saved her, silently pleading for mercy. It was all a mistake. She had been too careless and now she was sure to die for it. His grip tightened on her arm, warning her not to move.

"Halt!" His voice loud enough that only the solaks could hear him.

He waved his hand motioning for the soldier's to cease their advances. As he did so, a familiar pattern caught her attention. It was placed on a ring he wore on his forefinger. Tulips intertwined and wove themselves around the length of the band. An oval was set at the top of the ring where the pattern changed into ogival lattice covering the face of it. In the center was a round gemstone the color of dried cranberries. She'd seen this pattern before. It was on the locket Manula stored her tutku flower.

How odd, she mused, before meeting the glance of the strange soldier who still held her to him.

"Sheath your weapons," he ordered, his gaze never once leaving hers. "She's of no threat."

A breath she hadn't noticed she was holding escaped her lips, letting her lungs relax.

Why is he saving me? She wondered, cheeks flushing as she realized everyone was watching.

The solaks, though reluctant, finally lowered their arrows. Indignant murmurs flooded through the mass as they watched Emel pull from the soldier's grasp and disappear.

CHAPTER 2: Görücülük

The sun beat down on Timur's forehead forcing him to squint against the light. The solaks marched down the dusty streets, a difficult feet as humans lined the sidewalks on either side watching the sultan parade. The sultan held his head up high, his chest puffing as he played the part of a powerful leader, but it was all a facade. The power that emanated from him was solely for the crowd's behalf. They wanted a strong, fearless leader. Little did they know there was someone more powerful pulling at the strings.

Blood pulsing through the crowd's veins taunted Timur and he grimaced. He could still taste the thick and decadent blood caked to the roof of his tongue. He kicked himself for being so weak.

"Can't believe Ramadan will be upon us so soon. It makes their blood taste vile." Adel, his fellow solak and closest friend, nodded towards the crowd.

"Vile is what we are," Timur muttered in reply, keeping his pace aligned with the other solaks.

"I don't understand your self-loathing. Why wouldn't you want to be a solak?"

"Being a solak isn't the problem." Timur reminded him.

"Yeah, yeah, the title comes with a few other perks." Adel shrugged with a sheepish grin. "Trust me, being an Ubir is so much better than being human. You're lucky not to remember it."

Timur glanced down at Adel, who was nearly panting as he looked at the crowd like they were food.

"Right now their blood would taste..." He sucked in air, licking his lips. "Sweeter than spiced helva. In fact, I could eat a side of that while diving into their meaty necks."

Timur cringed at the thought of drinking from the vein. If it weren't for the fact that he required blood to survive, he wouldn't have anything to do with the whole business of it. It was a constant struggle having to fight against the instinct to kill, to take everything from another life. This was something he vowed never to do again. He would not kill to satisfy his thirst. The only killing he did was on the battlefield which, for a solak, would only happen if the sultan himself went out on campaign.

"You don't know what it's like to have always been this way," he shook his head, ashamed his only friend had accepted the life of Ubir so quickly.

"Before this I was nothing," Adel hissed. "A used rag. Now I'm a solak. The weakness I once had when you first met me was vanquished the moment I was turned."

"And you still don't remember who turned you?" Timur asked, curious to know if something had jogged his memory.

He'd never met another Ubir who could turn others like he could. It wasn't like he could ask his parents. He was an orphan, abandoned at a janissary camp to be raised by a secret group of elite Ubir soldiers. Whoever it was turning all of these people, the captain, the queen, the solaks, and all of the members of the Imperial Council had to be connected to him somehow. They could even be the ones that turned him. But he couldn't remember the transition, or ever being human for that matter.

"Nope." Adel shook his head. "And don't care to. I'm happy to call myself an Ubir. I'd rather be the hunter than the hunted."

A shriek caught Timur's attention and he turned to see a girl falling. He used all his strength to catch her before the humans could notice his sudden movement. Reaching her just in time, he pulled her back upright. When his eyes met hers, the blazing heat washed from his entire body.

A chill filled the air and iced over as he found himself pulled toward the ocean in her eyes. Glittered with golden tendrils, they curled into his heart and for once he didn't feel the thirst. Everything else disappeared as she consumed him.

His heart beat faster, goosebumps sweeping his arms. Was this what it was like to be human, he wondered?

"What are you thinking?" Adel spoke, his tone a volume only the Ubir could hear. "You could've exposed us!"

The sound of Adel's voice jolted him from his reverie, bringing him back to the reality that this woman was in trouble.

"Halt! Sheath your weapons. She's of no threat," he ordered the solaks to lower their weapons.

Although he knew they didn't approve of his life choices, they respected him as the oldest Ubir on the solak force. They could say what they wanted behind his back, but he wouldn't let them hurt this woman.

He reached for her hand, but she was already up on her feet. Fear spread across her face before disappearing into the crowd. She was gone, taking with her the fleeting sensation of humanity. The chilling security she brought vanished as swiftly as it had come, replacing it with the scent of blood rising from the hot earth. The sound of hearts beating pumped in his ears. The desire to feed took control as his canines throbbed. Swishing his tongue over the inflamed skin, the movement temporarily eased them as they threatened to extend. Her absence left him with a vengeful hunger and his heart ached at the loss.

"Back as you were," he growled at the staring solaks.

"Your weakness for humans will get you nowhere," Adel said, his eyebrows creased with concern.

"It's not a weakness," he replied as they continued to march in pace. "And whoever that was, she's not human."

***

"I can't believe that happened," Sidika cried as they neared their home.

Emel rolled her eyes. She had been repeating the same rant since they left in the middle of the parade.

"You could've been killed!"

"But I wasn't," Emel replied, waving it off, "I don't understand what the big deal is."

Sidika huffed, sputtering as if trying to find the right words to convince her she was right. She wasn't, of course.

When they made the turn into their courtyard Emel knew they were in trouble. Their mother stood at the door, a scowl on her face.

"Now you've done it," Sidika hissed. "You'll get us both in trouble."

"Yes, yes, I know." She sighed, waltzing towards Funda and the impending consequences of sneaking out.

"Careful," Sidika grabbed her arm before she was able to enter the courtyard. "We don't want to disturb Abzar İyesi. I can sense its protective presence."

"Seriously?"

"Shh!" Sidika warned, eying their mother.

"But we live here."

"Yes, well…" Sidika shrugged. "We're not supposed to be out. It could mistake us for intruders. It can take the form of any animal, remember? Like that snake curling around the pillar!"

"Come on," Emel replied, refusing to get pulled into such myths.

Sidika glanced from side to side before following her. With her head down low, Emel rushed down the stone-covered path as fast as she could.

"How dare you run off into the streets without anyone with you," Funda hissed, her smoky eyes revealing her concern. "Do you have any idea what might've happened to you?"

"I warned her not to!" Sidika squealed.

"I will have a word with you later." Funda glared at her younger daughter.

"We went for prayer," Emel said, hoping her mother didn't recognize her lie.

"You nearly missed a very important meeting," her mother retorted, ignoring her rebuttal. "To think what would've happened to this family if you had been missing a few minutes more? Misfortune would bring curses to your family."

"Who am I meeting today?"

"The news would have reached all the families by nightfall," her mother continued, her voice increasing in volume with each word.

An exasperated sigh escaped Emel, not fond of her questions left unanswered.

"You would've ruined Sidika's prospects, too." Her shrill voice in the distance.

Emel realized her mother and sister had already entered the house and rushed to catch up. Upon entering the sofa Manula and the other servants guided her into the bath.

"Do everything Evranaki tells you to," her mother warned, motioning to the head maid. "This meeting could very well set you for life. You caught the eye of the chief judge's wife. Her son might very well be on his way to becoming the youngest chief clerk ever seen."

"Lucky me," she said, her heart sinking.

"Yes, indeed." Funda smiled as if they agreed before leaving her to the task of bathing.

Manula gently nudged Emel into the tub. A gasp escaped her lips as the water wrapped itself around her toes.

"It's cold." She whimpered to Manula.

"Might've been warm had you made it back in time," Evranaki barked.

Manula looked more sympathetic to Emel's situation as she helped guide her further into the frigid water.

Despite the cold water treatment, this room was still one of her favorites. Its domed ceiling was made of glass, letting the light reflect on the water below. The bath itself was the shape of an octagon and painted a turquoise that could woo any heart into its depths. If she ignored the bustling women around her, she could almost believe that she was swimming in the ocean.

She closed her eyes, the warmth of the sun beaming down upon her. She fantasized that she was swimming in the ocean alone, free from the constraints of her kaftan and the stifling rules of etiquette. Here she could scream with joy, or cry with pain. She could let her feelings be heard. The excitement of such freedom set her heart to hammering in her chest.

She giggled as she envisioned a seabird flying by. She saw something bobble above the water for the briefest moment before sinking deep within the blue sea. Submerging herself entirely, she dove after the mystery leading her far away from her troubles. When she came up for air she was startled to meet the piercing stare of the soldier from the parade. His deep olive skin glistening as water beads dripped from his soaking black hair onto his sculpted chest. He stood before her, waist deep in the ocean water. She admired his square jaw and high cheekbones, his large lips slightly lifting at the corners into a smile.

"What are you doing in my dream?" She asked.

He provided no answer as he stepped closer, his warm fingertips brushing against her cheek. Her breath caught as his hands snuck their way through her knotted chestnut hair. The warmth of his palm wrapped around her neck, pulling her against him. A gasp escaped her lips as his hot breath met her ear.

"You are my security," his deep voice whispered.

She knew it was only her imagination, but it was a dream she hoped would never end. Only in her imagination would a man find safety in the arms of a woman.

"What is the matter with her?" Evranaki's voice startled Emel from her thoughts and the view of the washroom returned to her.

She forgot that she was inside the confines of a bathtub. Blinking several times, she hoped it all had not just been a dream. But the solak was gone, replaced with only the group of women staring suspiciously at her.

"Has she drunk the water?" Manula asked, her voice filled with worry. "She will surely be followed by misfortune."

"That is her concern now." Evranaki shrugged, bringing her a towel. "Come, Emel, or you'll be late."

Forced to leave the safety of her daydreams, Emel let them guide her out of the tub.

"I didn't drink any water, Manula," Emel said as she dried her long hair into neat waves.

"Oh, how wonderful." Manula sighed with relief. "For a moment I thought everything was ruined."

"Don't worry." She smiled, not wanting to shatter the myths Manula clung to.

"Drink," Evranaki ordered, pushing a cup of hot tea into her hands.

She gladly sipped its contents while they spun her into her finest gown. She felt the luscious velvet of the ruby fabric and admired the intricate tulips, made of golden thread, that weaved their way down the length of the robe. The red hue resembled the strength of fire, an element she knew to be worshiped among many. She wondered if this was a subliminal message for the mothers who would see her in it. What would this woman be like?

"Straighten your shoulders," Evranaki advised. "You'll never believe how many families are ostracized for less than a slouching beauty."

Emel shuddered at the thought. As much as she wanted to be free, she did not want her family, let alone her sister, to pay for it. Unfortunately her mother hadn't born a son. Women with sons were the luckiest as they held all the power. They were the only ones that could seek out a potential spouse. If the mothers proclaimed the girl a disgrace, this would lead her into a life of servitude. Emel's hands quivered at the thought of it, angering her spirit that wished to be free.

Pulling her shoulders upright, she lengthened her neck as high as it would go. For the sake of her sister, she would play the part.

For now, she promised herself as the maids guided her from the washroom.

Passing through the downstairs lounge, they entered the sofa where she would meet the chief judge's wife. It was a long rectangular room that stretched across the full length of the house. Wooden shutters covered the sun that usually shone through the bay windows facing the courtyard, casting the room with shadows. It would've looked gloomy, had it not been for the bright and vibrant cushions that filled the room with cheer.

The chief judge's wife did not look up as Emel entered, her scowled face clashing against the bright yellow and red carnation motifs that covered the cushion she sat on. The deep lines on her forehead told Emel that she had much unhappiness in her life. This did not bode well for this being a good match for her. Not that she had a say in any of it.

Emel tried her best to avert her gaze behind the sheer, golden veil. Yet her curiosity could not be helped. She did everything to calm herself as she was led closer to the rather plump-figured woman. Anger radiated from her body that Emel could see the putrid aura of hostility surrounding her.

Funda sat at the far end of the sofa. A quick glance in her direction told Emel that she needed to avert her gaze. Emel reluctantly lowered her head.

Loud slurping noises filled the room as the chief judge's wife sampled the quality of the coffee service.

"Humpf!" The noise escaped her pursed lips before she pushed herself up from her seat, cup still in hand.

She moved closer to Emel and it took all of her strength not to take a step back. There wasn't enough space in the world between her and this woman. Her gaze scraped against Emel's skin as she studied her from head to toe. Emel did not like being the center of this older woman's critical examination. It took all of her resolve not to pull on her knuckles. The discomfort that filled the room made her nerves tense.

"Remove the veil," the chief judge's wife ordered.

Her eyes darted to her mother, begging her to come to her aid.

Is this even allowed? Emel wondered, *how dare she even make such a request.*

There was no doubt in Emel's mind that the chief judge's wife could see her face clearly. Her veil was practically see through. It was a power play at best, the heavy woman was throwing around her authority trying to take advantage of her vulnerable situation. Raising her glance, she stared straight at the woman before her. The visible rage seething from her made the chief judge's wife raise a chunky eyebrow. She hoped her defiance would tell this woman that she was not afraid.

Many moments passed in silence. The chief judge's wife looked to Funda who gave her approval. Emel's heart fell to the deepest depths of the ocean. Her mother was supposed to protect her, to be her greatest confidante, but her actions revealed her true ambitions. It told her that Funda was more interested in the furthering of the family's reputation than in her daughter's feelings and well-being.

The chief judge's wife snatched Emel's shield from her face, the only protection she had. Their eyes met, anger for anger. The corners of the woman's thin lips curled into a sneer, proud that she had the advantage. She enjoyed being in control, which told Emel she probably demanded such domination at home. This was another reason for her growing list of why this arrangement was doomed. She would never be pushed into submission by this bully. She would fight for her freedom until the very end.

The bitter stench of the chief judge's wife wafted through Emel's nostrils, her hot breath down her neck causing chills to run down her arm. Emel wondered when she would ever finish her little cup of coffee so that she could leave. Without a word, the woman sniffed Emel like she was a strange food upon her plate. She seemed satisfied with what she smelled before abruptly placing her hands around Emel's waist.

"Humpf." The grating sound escaped the prospective mother-in-law once more before removing her hands.

"My Hamid likes a girl with more meat on her," the woman's shrill voice commented. "But that can be fixed, I suppose."

The words struck a nerve and it took all of Emel's might to keep from vomiting on her. Emel wanted to run to her room and cry. A helplessness she had never known seeped into her soul, crushing her romantic dreams.

If this woman decided on Emel then she would pass along the information to the chief judge to make arrangements with Emel's father. She would be married and forever live as a wife to the son of a horrid woman. If she didn't approve or spread rumors about her, Emel would become a dishonor to the family.

How could mother allow a meeting with someone so disgusting? She wondered, yet deep down she knew she could not blame Funda.

As a mother of only daughters, Emel knew that Funda had no power to stop any of it. Life was a giant game of Mangala, where mothers with sons held all the seashells.

With one last appraisal the chief judge's wife returned to her seat, her coffee cup clattering on its saucer signaling the end of the meeting. Evranaki rushed to Emel's side, escorting her from the room. As soon as they reached the staircase leading to the upper rooms, she pulled her arm from Evranaki's grasp and ran. Taking the steps two at a time, tears streamed down her cheek. This would be her life from then on.

CHAPTER 3: Divan-ı Hümâyûn

Timur and Adel flanked the sultan as they escorted him to the council chambers, the other solaks either ahead or behind for further protection. Not that the sultan ever needed to attend these meetings. He was more of an accessory to his mother, always leaning on her every word with a glazed over expression.

"Do you ever wonder why the queen keeps him human?" Adel asked, his voice impossible to be heard by the sultan or the other soldiers. Luckily none of the others were high enough in ranks to be Ubir. "It's risky to keep him guarded by us."

Timur rolled his eyes, wishing for once Adel would watch his tongue.

"The sultan should be pitied," Timur replied. "I can sense the toll the queen's constant compulsion is having on him."

"How can you tell?"

Timur glanced at Sultan Mustafa, whose rigid stride made him almost look lifeless. He could almost pass for an Ubir if it wasn't for his skin that reeked of salt.

"Look at the corners of his eyes," he said, indicating the subtle black spidery veins, a sign that was all too obvious to

Timur. He'd witnessed it many times on the battlefield. Their captain wielded this power over the lower-level soldiers to prevent their human weakness from showing. It was a strategy that helped build the empire, but destroyed many lives.

To the normal eye, the lines plaguing the sultan's could hardly be seen, so fine that they could've passed for bloodshot eyes if they weren't so dark.

"Only you would notice such a thing," Adel commented, shaking his head in disbelief. "Do you think she feeds on him?"

Timur shot him a warning look as they approached the chambers. The room would be filled with the council members, all of which were Ubir.

"I would feed on him," he continued.

He missed the days of their childhood, when the soldier before him was just a young little boy who took compassion on him. Adel was the only human he knew that could see the good in everyone. All of this changed when they grew up and Adel was turned. Timur didn't want to think about what made him so callous towards humans.

"If she truly loved her son, the queen would've had him turned by now."

"And lose her endless supply of food?" Adel asked. "Besides, I'm sure she would lose her power over the empire."

"Perhaps that would be for the best." Timur shrugged.

"Now who should be careful?"

They quickly put a stop to the conversation as they entered the dimly lit room, only the light from the small glass windows above and a few lanterns provided any light. A group of cushions were placed in the center of four pillars, Timur and the other guards took positions at each corner. As the nishanji's scribe passed him, the scent of his human blood caused his fangs to burn. He hoped the meeting wouldn't last very long. As much as he wished he didn't have to, he knew it was about time to feed.

The valide sultan, or Queen Naz as she was known to the Ubir, entered the room and moved swiftly to her throne. Her elaborate seat was placed at the head of the circle, perched slightly higher than the sultan himself. Her braided hair curled like snakes down her waist, clashing against her pasty complexion. Once all of the council members had taken their seats, her eyes flashed crimson indicating the meeting could commence.

"The territories of Hungary are where we must put our energies," the chief judge advised, "Only then will the empire have the capacity to grow further."

"Very good, Halil," Queen Naz agreed, addressing the judge directly.

Timur's suspicious vibes began to tingle at the mention of growth. Did this mean another round of promotions? This hadn't happened since Adel's transformation only a year ago. They seemed to be turning soldiers at a much more increase pace than before. This rate couldn't be sustainable. It was almost as if the queen wanted the entire army to be Ubir. That didn't sit well with him.

"With all due respect," the grand vizier spoke up, sitting proudly with his tall, rounded hat affixed majestically atop his head, "I believe that there are more pressing matters. Problems that lie a little closer to home that require our attention."

"Such as?" Naz asked, raising an eyebrow.

"The civil unrest among the Ubir factions has led many to starve and cut out the human supply in their rival's territories," the grand vizier explained, "If we do not address this we will risk a rebellion that could bring all of this to its knees."

"This is why we have the janissary captain," Chief Judge Halil retorted.

Timur could tell the grand vizier was visibly irritated at the judge, massaging his bearded chin in an attempt to soothe his disposition.

"They are to be patrolling the streets," the judge continued, "If there is disorder then he has full authority to deal with it then and there. That is, unless the agha is having difficulties doing his job."

Unable to control his frustration, a threatening hiss escaped the grand vizier as he revealed his pearly white fangs.

"Gentlemen." Queen Naz rose from her seat. "There's no need to fight."

A pulsating light flashed from her eyes, causing all the officials to relax. Timur wasn't sure what kind of blood she was drinking to receive such power, he had never seen an Ubir compel others as thoroughly as she could.

"Expansion is in all of our best interests. We will provide the agha with more soldiers to enforce civility," Queen Naz said. "If anyone threatens this, I trust the agha will know how to deal with them. I agree with chief judge. We must reclaim these lands if we are to provide enough sustenance for our Ubir brothers."

The mere thought of all the slaves that would become either food or entertainment to the Ubir left Timur with an indescribable pain. How many lives could he just stand by and watch them take? Didn't they have enough? Couldn't they get by like he did, only taking a small amount of blood without killing or forcing them into slavery? But he knew that this would never happen with Queen Naz as their leader. He could sense a darkness in her much greater than any monster. Her ways could only lead to destruction. He wondered how she could be stopped, with as much power as she seemed to have. There were many things he didn't know, but he knew for sure that Queen Naz would have to be stopped from following through with her plan for expansion.

"Let the orders be written," Queen Naz announced, motioning for Nishanji Hasan-Ali and his scribe to begin.

She turned her attention to the sultan and whispered something in his ear. His expression became unfocused and dazed. Soon he was reciting everything she instructed him to say.

"I, Sultan Mustafa, advise additional soldiers be delivered to the janissary agha." The sultan paused, the sound of the scribe's writing the only thing that echoed within the chamber.

He blinked, his mouth falling open yet no words escaped them. Life returned to his face, his eyebrows furrowing as he looked around the room in confusion.

"What is happening? Where am I?" the sultan asked, his voice much deeper than it had ever been before. "Who are you?"

Queen Naz's long, claws grasped his shoulders, turning him towards her.

"You're safe," she cooed, her gaze locked on the sultan who began to shake under her grasp.

"No, no, let me out!" The sultan screamed, the sudden noise making the scribe jump as he wrote every word down.

"Send your scribe away," the queen ordered before returning her focus to the sultan who was looking around frantically.

"Mustafa…," she whispered, the power in her voice demanding attention.

The sultan slowly turned to face the queen and Timur watched in awe as she compelled the hysterical sultan.

What was that all about? Timur wondered.

He knew that the queen compelled the sultan, but why would he know what was happening? Better yet, why would he ask who they were? He had never seen compulsion used this way and to the extent the queen had. Perhaps memory loss was a side-effect of long term compulsion? It was just a theory, one that Timur would not want to put to the test.

An awkward silence filled the room causing many to shift in their seats, uncomfortable with the turn of events. Out of the corner of Timur's eye, he could see the glazed expression return to the sultan, his focus far away.

"Let's finish this, shall we?" Queen Naz smiled sweetly, motioning for the scribe to return to his post.

"The agha will execute any and all disturbers of peace," the sultan's thin voice returned as the queen's compulsion took hold of him once more. "A plan to conquer the Hungarian territories will be prepared immediately by the chief judge. Following approval of such plan, a campaign will commence."

Timur could tell that the grand vizier was upset with this decision, but made no objections as the sultan's, or rather the queen's orders were written. When the scribe finished, both the sultan and the nishanji signed the document. This concluded the meeting, allowing all the officials to go and satiate their blood-thirst as the night had begun.

"Well, that was strange, wasn't it?" Adel said, coming up to join Timur.

"Indeed," he replied.

"Ready to break the fast?"

"Never, as always," he replied.

"Come on, let's get out of here." They nodded their acknowledgment of their replacements for the night as they headed towards the exit.

"Hold on," Timur said, his voice low as he spotted the chief judge and the nishanji whispering intensely barely out of earshot.

What business could the chief judge have with the nishanji? Usually they kept their distance from one another. It was odd to see them this engaged. They glanced over their shoulders before disappearing through the exit.

"What is it?" Adel asked.

It was most likely nothing to worry about. Perhaps they were just discussing the sultan's strange episode.

"Nothing." Timur shrugged.

"I don't know about you, but I'm starving."

"You go on, then." He urged.

"You're skipping again? You need to be careful not to starve yourself."

"Not tonight, but I have something else I need to do first."

"Suit yourself," Adel said before leaving.

Timur couldn't shake the feeling like something shady was going on between the chief judge and the nishanji. He would try his best to follow them and find out all he could. His thirst could wait. Or it would have to.

***

"What will you do if she does choose you?" Sidika sat on a large, silk cushion next to a line of bay windows overlooking the city. Normally this was Emel's favorite spot in the house as it was the only area where one could see the shore in the distance. But these days she was too upset to enjoy the scenery.

"I don't know, Sidika." Emel's eyes stung from the endless stream of tears. The anguish of being under the scrutiny of the chief judge's wife had lasted for days. The fear of being chosen plagued her heart and she desperately brainstormed a way to escape. So far she'd come up empty.

Sidika glanced out the window. "It's nearly sunset. Perhaps we could get the cooks to make us something sweet. It might make things better."

Emel looked at her beautiful sister and smiled. She always tried to find a way to cheer her up. Out of all of the siblings, Sidika was the only one she got along with. Being only two years apart in age, they had spent most of their life together.

"That sounds nice," Emel replied, stopping to gaze out the window as the sun set.

She admired the dark blues and pinks mixed with orange gleaming through the buildings as the last of the daylight hung on by a thread. It was her favorite time of day.

"Unless…" Emel's voice trailed as an idea formed.

"Unless what?"

Emel looked into her sister, hoping she wouldn't protest.

"Unless we sneak out and enjoy breaking the fast properly."

"No way. We will enjoy iftar safely. Here."

"Come on, it will be fun!"

"Like the last time we did that?" Sidika scoffed, referring to their outing to the bezesten. "It was a complete disaster! And what of the Ubir? They will surely be roaming the streets at night."

Emel rolled her eyes.

"It's a terrible idea. What if we get caught again? Or worse, served as the Ubir's dinner or kidnapped by slave traders?"

"You know very well that we could just as easily be kidnapped from our own beds than out there. At least then we would be living life instead of held up in this prison."

"That only happens to Armenians. It would never happen to us." Sidika protested, but Emel could tell she knew that this wasn't necessarily true.

"We will wear disguises this time." Emel headed for the cupboards that lined the room in search of a proper costume. She knew there had to be some extra fabric somewhere.

"You'll be going whether or not I go, won't you?" Sidika asked, her face etched with uncertainty.

"Of course."

Sidika's lips pursed, thoughtfully. Emel wished she would make up her mind soon. The night was upon them and she didn't want to miss any of the festivities that awaited them.

There would be so much to explore and Emel didn't want to miss a second of it.

"Please?" Emel batted her eyelashes, grasping her sister's hands. "It will be so much better exploring the city with you."

"Manula already got in trouble for letting us leave. And the other servants surely won't help this time."

"That shouldn't be a problem." Emel assured her sister. "Everyone will be too busy preparing the food for our parents."

Emel had everything figured out, she just had to convince Sidika to go along with it. Adventures were much more fun with company.

"But how will we go without being seen? I don't want to be harassed or have to worry about being put in danger."

"Don't worry," Emel smiled, the fluttering sensation of butterflies filled her delighted heart. "I've got a plan."

CHAPTER 4: The Köçek

The streets of Constantinople, nightfall.

Timur cursed himself for losing sight of the two officials. He had followed them from the palace, but once they reached the streets they quickly disappeared. He would have to keep his eyes and ears open at future meetings. He couldn't quite put his finger on it, but something strange was going on.

The city was alive with hungry fasters finding food and drink to satisfy them. Reaching for his ring, he opened the locket to find the last of his tutku flower. He brought the herb to his nose, inhaling the fruity scent with hints of grass. The aroma dulled the ache in the pit of his stomach, but he knew it wouldn't be enough. His fingers quivered as hunger took over him. He loathed himself as he trudged through the bustling streets, looking for someone to turn down a dark alley by mistake.

He was glad to be away from Adel. He often lacked the self-control to stop once he latched on. Timur could not let himself be around that kind of temptation. His body craved what his mind knew was not right. He would only take enough to survive.

The scent of warm simit wafted through the air, putting a smile on Timur's face that was normally lined with worry.

I shall have some after I gain my strength, he thought.

The idea left him with a joyous sorrow. He longed for a life where a simple loaf of bread would satisfy his hunger. He longed for the moments where he could indulge himself without the feeling of pure guilt. Without the awareness of the monstrosity that he was.

A young heartbeat pulled him from his thoughts, drawing his attention. He slipped around an old man with graying hair, his senses guiding him towards his target. Pushing himself through the crowd, his gaze fell on a köçek, his strangely large turban bouncing as he danced to a beat of his own. The man looked very out of place, only accompanied by one other dancer. It was a very unusual sight as they normally danced in large groups.

Their lively movements captivated Timur, a smile crawling upon his face as they bobbed their heads, making faces to taunt the growing crowd. The twirling of the symbols in their hands caught his eye and he couldn't help but think at how feminine they looked. Köçek were often known to try and mimic the movements of women, but these men had outdone themselves.

It was all good fun, until they ran into a group of Albanians. Their bulky frames were built like warriors and they glared down at the two small dancers, before pushing them aside without another word. Timur let his nervous breath go as he watched the two get separated. Smiling, he raced towards the alley the taller dancer stumbled into. The dark breezeway between the wooden buildings arched on either side, the sounds of the busy street fading into the background.

Timur crept closer to the dancer who was adjusting his disheveled turban. With one swift move, his fists wrapped around the man's skinny shoulders, pinning him against the stone wall. A high pitched shriek escaped before he secured his palm over the dancer's mouth. When he gazed down at his captive, a feeling of awe washed over him when he recognized the dancer's true identity.

Timur studied the irises with golden flecks that were staring fearfully back at him. It was her. The woman from the crowd. The need for blood drained from his body as a cool calmness washed over him. The ache in his stomach vanished and all he could pick up was the scent of rosewater on her neck.

A slight pinched feeling came from his palm, he realized she was trying to bite him. Letting go of her, he backed away as a sudden fit of laughter overcame him.

"You laugh?" She cried.

He looked at her, holding his chest as he tried to compose himself. This was not like him at all. He never laughed like that before. Then again, he had never had the burden of his bloodlust lifted from him.

"I'm so sorry. I'm just surprised to see you."

"What do you mean?" She demanded. "You follow me into the alley, pinning me as if I'm some sort of animal. Do you even know who I am?"

"A dancer, of course." He teased.

Her eyebrows furrowed, a look of contempt spreading across her face.

"What? You don't think I am?"

"Well, I know you aren't male," he replied.

She opened her mouth to respond only to shut it when a light flickered through the night sky. Her eyes grew wide, as if she were only now realizing who he was.

"It's you!" she gasped, bringing her fingers up to her turban. "The solak."

"And you," he said, motioning to her. "The woman who fell at the parade."

"Thanks for reminding me."

"I didn't mean it like that," he quickly replied. "You just left in such a hurry before I could ask if you were alright."

"I am." She shrugged. "A little fall couldn't hurt me."

The corners of Timur's lips curled ever so slightly. Her fearless confidence was like no other he had ever known and it only drew him closer.

"Why did you save me?"

"That's difficult to explain," he said. "I guess you could say it's something about those beautiful eyes of yours."

A brilliant smile grew from ear to ear across the woman's face. She quickly lowered her gaze as if embarrassed, her cheeks flushing.

"And why have you grabbed me now?" she asked, shifting her stance nervously.

His heart skipped a beat at her question. He didn't want her to fear him. He desired nothing more than to protect her from the harsh reality of the Ubir's existence. Unfortunately, this meant he would have to keep her as far away from him as possible.

"I-I thought you were someone else," he stuttered. "There have been disturbances all through the city and when I saw you duck away from the crowd I thought—"

"I didn't duck into the alley on purpose. If you hadn't noticed, I was separated from my sister."

She grimaced, as if kicking herself for giving away too much information.

"I'm very sorry," he replied, bowing his head. "I didn't mean to disturb you."

A painful silence set between the two and Timur wished he could read the expression on her face. He could hear the nervous pitter-patter of her heart and desired nothing more than to hold her in his arms and soothe her distress. Yet, this was not an option. He couldn't allow himself to get too close to her.

"I guess I can forgive you," she finally replied. "Simple misunderstanding. I shall just be on my way, then."

Panic swept his heart when she turned to leave. As the distance grew, the gut-wrenching craving returned. He cringed as the scent of blood filled the air and the emptiness Emel once filled returned. How could one woman have so much power over him? He knew he would have to let her go, but did that have to be tonight? He then realized it was too late, he had already let himself get too close to her.

"Wait!" He exclaimed, running to catch up.

When their eyes met, the emptiness vanished as swiftly as it had materialized. Against his better judgment, his heart prayed to never part from her.

"Allow me to help you," he said, hoping this would buy him more time.

"No, thank you," she replied. "It was very nice to see you, but I can manage."

Watching her walk away required much restrain as the vicious burning took hold of him. The strength of his bloodlust knocked him to his knees. What kind of evil spirit was she? Taunting him with the freedom he could only hope for.

***

Emel quickened her pace, not wanting to be in the shadows any longer. She tried to push the feelings the solak had stirred within her out of her mind, but the bouquet of spiced berries, amber, and musk lingered making it an impossible feat. The memory of his warm breath against her cheek distracted her from the fear she'd felt when he'd first grabbed her.

Shaking the images of his curly hair falling into his intense eyes from her mind, she focused on finding Sidika. How did they get separated?

"We were standing right next to each other when the giants pushed by us." She reviewed. "Sidika can't be too far, right?"

She desperately hoped that this was true as she stepped out onto the main street to retrace her footsteps. Her gaze darted from one turban to the next, yet each face that came into view didn't belong to her sister. Panic set in as she feared the worst. A cloudy haze crept into her vision. She batted away the tears that threatened as she shoved her way through the throngs of men.

"Watch it!" A gruff man shouted as she knocked into his shoulder.

"Sorry," she mumbled, pushing past him.

The man's look changed after she spoke. She hadn't taken care in disguising her voice! She quickened her pace, hoping to blend in with the crowd. She was overcome by a sensation that someone was watching her and she knew she was being followed. Her heart pounded as she scanned the streets for a place to hide. Yet, each corner revealed dark paths she refused to go down. She didn't want to be trapped in an alley with another strange man. Chances were the second time would not go as well for her.

Where is Sidika? She groaned.

What if she was captured by traders? They would never get her back then. Her stomach launched into her throat, glancing over to find the man was right on her tail. His scowling face was locked on her and she knew he would not stop until he had her.

Why did she want to come out here in the first place? They could've been enjoying dates from the comfort of their own room. Instead, she had to go and choose the more adventurous choice. It was all her fault.

Pushing through a group of people in line for fresh simit, she suddenly saw a short turban donning dancer. It had to be her.

"Sidika!" She cried, but her shouts were quickly silenced when a hand covered her mouth.

Strong arms pulled her into a dark side street. Everyone around her was so preoccupied with the feast they didn't notice her being taken. Kicking against the body behind her, she quickly found her arms being secured to her sides.

"Now, let's see who you really are," the man's voice wheezed, causing her to cringe.

Spinning her to face her abductor, his pudgy face was a mere inch from hers. He reeked of spoiled food and clothes that hadn't been washed in some time.

"Tie her wrists," he ordered, licking his lips.

Peering over her shoulder, she saw a group of men creep out from the shadows. A sob escaped her lips as one of them grabbed her hands, securing them behind her. After the man who had grabbed her was satisfied that she would not be able to get away, he reached for her turban. She bit down on his hand that covered her mouth, satisfied that he was not as strong as the solak when her bite drew blood.

"Ow!" the pudgy man howled, pulling his hand away to nurse it.

He glared at her, and the back of his other hand slammed into her face. The blow causing her to stumble to the ground.

The cold stone broke her fall, unable to catch herself with her hands tied.

"You'll be sorry for that," he said. "Gag her."

"No!" she cried, trying to pick herself up.

She had to find a way out. Firmly shutting her mouth, she fought against the piece of cloth one of them was attempting to force on her. This couldn't be happening. She regretted not taking the solak up on his offer to help find Sidika. Perhaps if she hadn't been so stubborn she wouldn't have been in this mess.

Strong fingers pushed into her cheeks, forcing her jaw to rise like a dog. The nauseating flavors of sweat filled her mouth as they tied the gag around her.

"There, that's better." The man grinned.

The plump leader ripped the turban from her head allowing her long waves to tumble out of the cloth. Lust filled his expression as he gazed upon the golden brown strands that reached down to her waist.

"Would you look at that." He sneered, causing bile to rise in Emel's throat. "With that mane and those eyes, you'll sell quite nicely."

He grabbed her arm, pulling her to her feet and led her farther into the darkness. Tears stung as they spilled upon her cheeks. All she wanted was to find her sister and go home, but how could that happen now?

A harsh breeze that smelled of spices and fruit blew by her causing a chill to run down her arm. The chubby man next to her was suddenly nowhere to be seen. Piercing screams filled the night air as one by one, each man that surrounded her vanished. She turned to run, but her foot caught a jagged rock causing her to tumble to the ground once more. She grimaced, preparing for the pain her fall would cause. Yet it never came. Something had caught her just before her face smacked against the ground. Strong arms pulled her upright. Her breathing increased as fear grasped her heart. She enjoyed adventure, but she was nearing her limit.

CHAPTER 5: Don't Fear the Ubir

"It's okay," a deep and fruity voice melted like chocolate in her ear.

Emel's heart skipped a beat as she recognized the scent of berries that filled the air. She wondered what made him smell so wonderful all the time. Opening her eyes, she met the solak's gentle, yet intense gaze.

"You're safe." He assured her, his fingers brushing against her cheek as he unfastened the fabric across her mouth.

Licking her lips, the taste of iron reached her tongue as she licked the corners of her lips where the rough fabric had cut her.

Grimacing, she looked up at the solak in time to see rubies appear within his irises.

"How can you do that?" She asked, unable to look away.

"Do what?" The solak soldier asked.

She blinked and the crimson jewels in his eyes vanished, but she knew she hadn't imagined it.

"They change colors so quickly, from red to bronze."

Averting his eyes from hers, he began examining her wounds. An awkward silence fell between the two and she could sense his reservation.

Emel continued to study the man before her. He had attacked her once, apparently by accident, yet saved her twice. Her first instinct told her it was a romantic gesture just like she had always dreamed of.

But how did he find you? A little voice in her head that sounded more like Sidika than herself asked. *Was he following you this whole time? What if Sidika's right about the monsters?*

Sidika. She was still missing, Emel desperately had to find her. How could she forget so quickly? Had she hit her head that hard?

"Thank you, but I must go," She insisted.

"I know, you must find your sister." He had remembered. "I can help with that, but let me first take care of your wounds."

"Why are you doing this? H-how did you find me?" She stammered, unable to hold back her questions.

Bright, russet eyes sparkled in the night sending butterflies swarming her insides. He looked down at her wrists, carefully unwinding the rope.

"I heard your cries," he whispered, massaging the bruises from her wrists.

"How?" She asked, more curious than afraid. "And what happened to those men?"

She knew her sister would tell her to run away, but something about him drew her closer. Wanting to find out more about who he was, how he could move faster than the wind. He could've been dangerous, but nothing about him made her afraid. His expression begged her to run, but the touch of his warm hands urged her to stay. The solak's sculpted chest beckoned for her to rest her head and never leave the safety of his arms. She didn't want to think about anything beyond this. Life was too short to worry.

"Hold still." His eyes searched hers for permission before wrapping the palms of his hands on either side of her head, his thumbs resting on her temples.

With eyes shut to the world, the rhythm of his breath slowed. A tingling sensation nestled in the center of her chest, growing like ivy through her veins. It spread down her arms, sealing up her wounds until each cut and bruise were healed removing all physical evidences of the men's attack. The pain washed away like dirt running from a storm.

"How do you feel?" He asked, carefully watching her reaction.

"Amazing." A sigh of relief escaped her.

Who was this man? How could he be real? Her head must've hit the ground hard for it to imagine all of this.

"How did you do that?"

"Come on." His warm hand wrapped around hers and sent her heart fluttering. "We should get out of here before they come back."

"Come back? I thought you took care of them?"

"I did, but they still have use of their legs." The solak's full lips curled at the corners into what might pass for a smile. It dissolved as quickly as it materialized, the solak lowering his gaze.

"Why didn't you take those, too?" The thought of those men still walking around left a nauseous pit in her stomach.

His laughter bounced between the dark homes that flanked them, his body shaking as a true smile exposed sharp canines. Emel couldn't help but giggle at the sound of it coming from the giant warrior before her.

"You are truly surprising," he commented, picking up her tattered cloth turban from the cobblestone street.

Wrapping it around her head, his fingers lingered at the corners of her eyelids. Before she could say anything, his hands were gone. It took everything within her not to groan, as she desperately wanted to be in his arms once more.

"Let's figure out what happened to your sister, shall we?"

"But how can we?" It was another question left unanswered as the strange man guided her away from the bustling market street and further into the night.

She ignored the inner voice that urged her to run. She would never run from an adventure.

"In order for me to sense your sister's whereabouts, I'll need to go somewhere quiet, preferably high up."

Raising an eyebrow, she glanced skeptically back up at him.

"I know this is a lot to take in," he said, recognizing her doubt. "I promise to explain as much as I can, but trust me. I will find your sister."

The sincerity in his voice reassured Emel that she was in good hands.

"If you think you can find my sister, I trust you." She smiled.

"When I say I'll need to be high up I do mean very high." His brow creased with concern. "Will you be alright with that?

"To find my sister? Of course! Besides, I've always liked challenging my fear of heights." She winked.

An uncomfortable smile played at the corners of his lips, as if he had never heard a joke before.

"I will need to carry you."

"Carry me? Why? My legs work fine," Emel was suddenly very confused by the abrupt announcement, not that she was complaining.

"I may run… a bit fast for you to keep up."

"How fast?" A thought began to prickle in Emel's mind. Perhaps this soldier was not quite as human as he looked. Yet, what else could he be?

"Please, don't fear me." She looked up into his pleading eyes. "I promise I will keep you safe."

"How could I fear you?" She asked, her heart thrilled by the thought of being in his strong arms. "You have saved my life. Twice. I trust you will help me find my sister safe and sound. I just have one question, and you must promise to answer."

"What might that be?" The soldier raised a thick eyebrow.

"Who are you?"

"My name is Timur," he offered, brushing a stray curl behind his ear. "I'm a solak for the sultan."

"No, not that. I mean, what are you?"

A lovely, dimpled smile spread across his tanned face.

"I believe that would be two questions."

"That's unfair." Emel bit her lip to keep from laughing. "I didn't get the answer that I wanted."

"I'll tell you what." The restraint left his demeanor as he removed the distance between them. "If you give me your name, you can ask me all the questions in the world. All I ask is that we first ensure your sister is safe."

"Technically, those are two things you have asked." Emel teased. "But I can't argue with it. I have to find Sidika."

Without another word, the soldier snuck his arm around her waist, sweeping her into his arms as if she were the lightest thing in the world.

"What are—?" Emel didn't get a chance to finish the question before he was running down the street.

Buildings blurred by them as Timur's legs moved at an incomprehensible speed. They travelled faster than humanly possible, the wind blowing Emel's hair into hundreds of gilded tangles.

Wind rushed through her ears, her breath caught as everything whirled by her like a dream. The wood and adobe homes flew past, their lights blurring into a long strand of yellow trailing behind them. They were heading farther away from the light, the sounds of the crowded marketplace was drowned out by the sounds of rushing wind.

The soldier lunged into the air, catching Emel by surprise as the ground disappeared below them. They soared up towards the heavens, the stars in the night sky the only thing providing any light.

"Hold on," Timur whispered in her ear, his even breath clashing with the fact that he had been running with her in his arms for what seemed like miles.

"What—?" She tried to ask, but her voice was replaced with delightful screams as they fell into darkness.

Her heart leaped into her chest, the free falling sensations making it impossible to speak.

The solak landed lightly on the ledge of a stone covered tower, high above the ground. Emel was dizzy, everything was still spinning from the motion. She needed to sit down.

Taking a step, an arm quickly slinked around her waist pulling her back.

"Careful," Timur warned.

Her eyes began to adjust, the moon beating down on them providing just enough light. The ground was far below them, much too far to be balancing on what had to be the tiniest ledge.

"Where are we?" She asked.

"Shh." He closed his eyes as if he were listening for something, his strong arm still around her waist.

The chill of the night wind blew his chin-length curls away from his square jaw, locked in concentration. Emel took this opportunity to take in their surroundings. There were several other towers just like the one they were balancing on. In the middle of the towers, small domed roofs jetted out from the building leading up to the center dome. Emel then realized where they were.

"It's the mosque," she said in awe, appreciating its grandeur even more from this angle.

Timur gave a single nod, never once opening his eyes. Emel watched him, a bit confused. What was he doing? Minutes went by in silence until, finally, he opened his eyes, his gaze locking onto hers.

"Your sister is safe," he said, his warm breath comforting her.

"How can you know this?" she asked, pushing away from his iron shoulders.

She couldn't think clearly being that close to him and the intoxicating aromas he exuded.

"I-I can hear her," he replied, uncertainty filling his eyes.

"Not that this hasn't been exciting, because I've rather enjoyed the ride, but I need to know how you know Sidika is alright?"

The ferociousness of her retort tugged at the corners of his lips.

"She's currently asking your maid if you've made it back yet," he explained.

"What's her name?"

"Sidika," he replied.

"No, not my sister's name, I've already told you that. I mean, what is the maid's name?"

"Manula."

Emel's jaw fell open, dumbfounded. How could he know this? She couldn't remember mentioning Manula in any of their conversations. Excitement beat recklessly deep within her heart as she pieced together what this Timur could be. She knew she should be afraid, but it was all too thrilling. Here was a man who had the power of a beast, yet the body of a janissary soldier. It would be a waste to let worry drown out the exhilaration of seeing life through his perspective. Plus, he had every opportunity to hurt her and hadn't. That had to count for something.

"And what's my name?" She asked, knowing she hadn't told him.

"I believe you were going to tell me?" He grinned sheepishly.

"And I'm sure you already know it somehow." She prodded.

His gaze shifted from hers, a sadness washing over them like waves crashing on a sandy shore.

"Fine, you can deny it." She shrugged, looking up into his eyes once more. "I'll go ahead and tell you what I know you already know. My name is Nishanji Hasan-Ali kizi Emel. I may even have a power of my own, because I'm fairly certain I know what you are."

Timur's head whipped back to look at hers. It was his jaw's turn to drop. A smile spread across Emel's face, she enjoyed surprising him for once.

"You're an Ubir."

His jaw clenched as if he were unsure of how to process her words.

"Aren't you?" She asked, raising an eyebrow.

She watched him as he absently caressed the ring on his forefinger with his thumb, reminding her of how Manula would reach for her locket.

"I've seen this pattern before." She gently touched the cold brass ring, her fingers lingering on his warm hand.

Timur looked down at his ring before meeting her curious gaze.

"Our maid keeps tutku flower in a locket with this same design."

"You know of tutku flower?" He seemed shocked by this.

"Yes." She nodded. "Manula's been putting it in our tea for years. It has a very earthy taste with hints of berry. I rather like it, actually. Is that what you keep in your ring?"

"It's getting late," he replied, avoiding her question. "I should get you back home."

Emel frowned as he pulled her into his arms once again.

"But you haven't answered any of my questions yet."

He looked at her, his expression begging her for understanding.

"Please forgive me for what I must do," he whispered.

Bright crimson radiated from Timur's irises, blinding Emel. She couldn't make out his words as they faded. Everything around her turned red, her thoughts spun out of control until she couldn't make anything out. When she opened her eyes they were standing in front of the courtyard to her home. Only a few lights flickered from within and she knew her sister must've been worried sick.

The solak looked down at her, his arms still around her waist.

"How are you?" He asked.

"I'm…" she furrowed her eyebrows as she tried to pinpoint how she was feeling.

There was something she was forgetting, but what could it be? All of her memories from that evening were jumbled, spinning around on their own and making it difficult to recall what happened.

"I'm fine, I think," she replied, trying to shake the unsettled feeling. "Thank you for your help, Timur."

How did she know this name? She remembered the man before her. He was the solak from the parade and had even saved her from the traders who nearly took her. But had he ever introduced himself to her?

"Goodnight." She waved, leaving before the soldier had a chance to reply.

CHAPTER 6: Confusion at the Palace

Outside the sultan's bedchamber.

Timur stood guard, restless and uncomfortable with the stillness. After ensuring Emel was safe and sound, he'd nearly forgotten it was his shift as bedchamber warden. A task he was certain a mere cadet would excel at.

A loud rumbling filled the vast hallway. It took him a minute to realize it was coming from his stomach, moaning for something of the iron variety. Oh, what he wouldn't give to be in the presence of Emel once more! With a bat of her stunning eyelashes she could wash his blood-thirst away. But it wasn't just this that kept his thoughts returning to her. It was her trusting nature, something that never came easy for Timur. How could she believe, after all she knew of the Ubir, that they could be anything else but monsters? How could she not be afraid of him? She was like no other he had ever met, human or otherwise.

He wondered how she could have the ability to remove his bloodlust. Perhaps this was the human reaction of taking tutku flower? It was curious that their maid even knew about the herb in the first place. Perhaps this meant that she wasn't the only one. Who had thought to give tutku flower to humans?

No matter if there were others who could rid himself of the bloodlust, he couldn't get Emel from his thoughts. Perhaps it was her adventurous ways, or how she had somehow known what he was and didn't seem to be afraid. It was an acceptance he had never experienced before. He kicked himself for letting her go, but what other choice did he have? Whatever she was, human blood still boiled within her and it was only a matter of time before his nature would end up hurting her.

It's better she never knew me, he tried to convince himself, but devastation clung to him at the formation of these words.

But didn't she remember your name even after compelling her to forget? He asked himself.

He replayed his steps, running through exactly how he'd locked onto her mind, picking out the memory of him exposing what he truly was. Sure, he was weak from fasting but removing human memories that were only a few minutes old was easy. It should've been, at least. And it seemed to have worked, except that she still remembered his name. Was this a side effect of the tutku flower as well? His heart burned at the memory of his name escaping her lips with a longing he'd never known before.

"STAY AWAY FROM ME!" A frantic voice jolted Timur from his musings.

A shudder rippled down the wall he stood against, alerting him to the raucous coming from behind the sultan's door. The dark hairs of his forearm prickled as he barged into the dimly lit chamber, his fingers itching to draw his weapon. The open window was the first thing that drew his attention. Then to the fluttering cloth curtaining the bed, but the room was still. Treading with care, he moved deeper into the space, drawing a small dagger from his belt. His hands desired to pull out his bow, but the dagger was a much better weapon at close range.

The medallioned silks that lined the walls muted the shattering of glass of a vase. A shard slid across the maroon tiled floor, hitting into the soft fibers of his right boot. Looking in the direction it had come from, he met the fearful gaze of the sultan's chief escort crouched behind the bedside cupboard. But why was she hiding?

A hand landed upon Timur's shoulder, but only for a moment. He gripped his attacker's fist, using his momentum against him as he flipped the intruder onto his back.

"What have you done with my mother?" The question came from the man he pinned to the floor.

His eyebrows furrowed, startled that he recognized the voice.

Timur peered at the intruder, the man's eyes were spattered with black veins. His irises were covered with a white film giving him the appearance that he was dead. The rusty brown of his beard and the sharp point of his nose exposed the intruder's identity. It was the sultan.

Timur removed the knife he threatened to plunge into the neck he thought was his enemy.

"Your Majesty!" He gasped, extending his hand to help Sultan Mustafa to his feet, but the sultan did not accept it.

Fear and panic struck the sultan as pushed himself away from Timur.

"You've taken her, haven't you?" The sultan screamed, sweat beading across his distressed brow.

"What? No, it's me. Timur. Here, let me help you," he stretched his hand out once more, carefully inching forward.

The sultan shuddered at the movement.

"Where's my father?" The sultan's voice was much too small for such a grown man.

"Your father?" Sultan Mehmed had died when Mustafa was a child.

The door to the room abruptly swung open and a dark figure emerged.

"You may go," the harem's chief spoke, his words more of an order than a suggestion.

"I thought there was an intruder," Timur tried to explain, sheathing his weapon. "The sultan doesn't seem to know where he is or who he is. He asked for his father!"

The kizlar chief picked the delusional sultan up from the heap on the floor, all while glaring at Timur.

"Unhand me!" Sultan Mustafa's voice shook as he looked up at the chief. "Oh, good. It's you. This woman is the one who did it."

The sultan's pudgy forefinger shook towards his chief escort. Timur couldn't help but think the sultan should have recognized her over the kizlar chief. How long had the queen been using compulsion on this poor man?

"She took my mother and I'm sure this man has something to do with it, too," the sultan insisted.

"Your assistance is not needed here," the chief said, frowning at Timur who stood stubbornly in his way. "You are dismissed. You, too."

The familiar tug of the chief's compelling command sent shivers down Timur's spine. From the strength of it he could tell the chief was fully fed. The woman couldn't get out of the room faster, but Timur was not a human like her. He thought about pulling the last bit of his strength to stand his ground, but he knew better. Any sign of disrespect towards the eunuch could get him killed.

Bowing his head low, he swiftly left the room. He couldn't shake the sight of the sultan's dazed expression. And what was all that about his mother being taken?

"No, they must be stopped," the sultan shouted, forcing Timur to turn back towards the open chamber door.

The kizlar chief gripped the sultan's arm in an iron fist as he pulled him down the hall. Timur ducked into a shadow, hoping the chief couldn't sense his presence. An urge to follow him sprung into his mind and his body slithered forward, his curiosity getting the better of him.

Creeping through the darkness, he was careful to keep a safe distance from the chief. They made their way through a long corridor, entering another wing. At the end of the hall, gold plated pillars lined a double-door entrance which opened on its own.

"What is all this shouting?" A melodic voice sang through the opening.

The slender form of Queen Naz slunk through the doors, her braids perfectly pinned atop her head. Her eyes flickered crimson at the sight of the chief half carrying the sultan, his arms flailing in protest.

"No, no, don't take me to her! I beg you!" The sultan cried.

The queen's nose crinkled, sniffing the air around them. She peered past the chief just as Timur ducked behind a corner. Holding his breath, his hammering heart screamed in protest.

"Do you smell that?" The queen asked.

"Smell what?" The kizlar chief replied.

"It smells... it smells like someone else is here. Were you followed?"

"AHHHHH!" The sultan's screams filled the hall. Timur sighed with relief, thankful the sultan had provided a distraction from his scent. He took this opportunity to sneak a peek from behind his hiding spot.

The valide sultan rolled her eyes. "Would he just shut up already?"

"He requires your compulsion," the chief informed.

"Of course he does," the queen's angular face twisted in mockery.

"This is the third time his memories have returned this week."

"I know, Bayar," she hissed, addressing the kizlar chief directly before turning her attention to the sultan.

"You're in luck, my sweet boy," she cooed. "I've just had a nice little snack and now I'm strong enough to help you. You don't have to feel this pain anymore, I will take this pain from you."

Timur frowned, wondering what the valide sultan could mean by this. The chief pushed the sultan to his knees before stepping back as the queen planted her right hand at the center of the sultan's forehead.

"Be still my child...," her voice curled through the air sending hissing vibrations reverberating through Timur's soul. He was certain every nearby Ubir could feel the power radiating from her words. "You're not in danger—you know you are safe with me. Forget what is troubling you."

It took all of Timur's might not to run to the sultan's aid, but he kept still. Then it stopped, the man's body once again still. The confusion fled from the sultan's face with the tears that blanketed his cheeks.

"Mama?" The sultan asked, his eyebrows furrowed as he looked around.

"Yes, my dear." Queen Naz smiled.

"How did I get here?"

"You don't remember?" The queen asked, looking pleased with the effects of her power. "You were asking for me. So the kizlar chief brought you here."

Mustafa paused, blinking as if this would aid in recollecting the memories she took from him.

"No," he stood to his feet, straightening the robe over his ample stomach. "I don't know what came over me. I shall leave you to your rest, Mama."

"That's a good boy." The queen smiled as he kissed her cheek.

"Goodnight." He sighed, rushing towards the archway Timur was standing behind.

Timur swiftly ducked his head back, pushing himself into the furthest corner behind a tapestry covering the wall with its golden tulip pattern. The movement shook dust from the fabric loose, tickling his nose. His lungs contracted, forcing air down his throat.

The sultan's head turned towards the startling noise. Timur held the sneeze in, refusing to breath. Thankfully the sultan shrugged it off and continued on his way. Timur exhaled, relieved and thoroughly ready to go back home and sleep. Peering from behind the carpet, he sensed the queen and the chief were nearby. He would just have to wait it out.

"Soon I fear he will be immune to your compulsion," Bayar cautioned as they walked down the hall.

"You don't have to constantly remind me of this," she snapped, stopping right in front of Timur's hiding spot.

Resting her hands on the railing, she gazed out over the lower level, watching as the sultan returned to his room.

"I'm much too weak and I'm running out of time," she whispered.

The chief towered above the queen, his slender fingers resting on her shoulder. She looked up at the chief, her eyes filled with what Timur could only describe as affection.

"You are not weak," Bayar murmured. "It was your strength that pulled me from those slave traders."

"But I was too late," she replied, her voice tinged with disgust. "I was too late to stop them from doing what they did to you."

"Naz, my queen…"

The devotion in Bayar's voice made Timur shift uncomfortably. He was certain no one knew the valide sultan and the kizlar chief had a history outside of the Harem. No one alive, at least.

"Without you I wouldn't be here," Bayar brushed his fingertips along the queen's shoulder.

"Oh, Bayar," the queen smiled gingerly up at the chief.

"You look at me as if you love me," he whispered, moving closer.

Queen Naz turned towards the chief, welcoming his warmth against her.

"You do things for me no one else can," she replied, her fingertips tenderly caressing Bayar's dark cheekbones as she admired his features.

"Let me feel again," he pleaded, folding his hands around hers. "Compel me as you've done before."

The corner of the queen's lip curled wickedly, delighting in his passion.

"You know my desires lie elsewhere," she whispered, rising to her tiptoes to nibble on his earlobe. "Bring me the maid-in-waiting and I shall give you your heart's desire."

Bayar's eyes flickered with greedy anticipation before swiftly leaving in search of her request. Timur couldn't take another minute of this. He needed to find a way out, watching carefully as the valide sultan turned to leave. Making sure the queen was out of earshot, he pushed himself from behind the dusty rug. Returning safely to his barracks was the only mission he would be on for the remainder of the night.

CHAPTER 7: Söz Kesimi

Home of Nishanji Hasan-Ali.

"You left me!" Sidika was furious, treading a hole into the middle of the dull, green-tea colored rug. The diamond medallion lattice was fading with age and neglect. Their mother swore the color brought her bad luck, which ensured them privacy most days.

Emel hadn't had a chance to talk to Sidika after getting back. She had fallen asleep as soon as she entered the room. Yet, from the moment she awoke her sister was demanding answers. Answers Emel could not for the life of her remember.

"Why didn't you come back for me?"

"Of course I came back for you," Emel replied, hurt that her sister would think she hadn't.

"And?" Sidika prodded.

"And what?" Emel asked, plopping down at their window seat, open to the morning breeze.

"What happened to you?"

Emel tried to replay the events from the night before. She remembered dancing, being pushed into the alleyway and then... nothing. It was like her memories were all running away, leaving behind gaps.

"I'm not sure what happened in the alleyway," she replied, honestly a bit scared at the thought of the time she was missing. "When I left the alley there were these men they… they realized my disguise wasn't real."

"Oh no," Sidika gasped, all signs of irritation fleeing from her face as she squeezed into the only space left on the embroidered cushion. "Did they hurt you?"

"I fell and…" she tried to speak fast, the blanks beginning to overpower any recollection of the night before she had left. "And then things go dark for a bit. I remember seeing these red circles floating in the air, they looked like eyes, and the smell of fruit. Yes, there was definitely this scent of berries in the air."

Emel smiled at the delightful smelling memory until the image of a pudgy man ripping her turban from her head flashed before her.

"These men caught up to me. I can still feel their leader's wheezing breath on my neck," she shuddered, absently massaging her wrists.

Sidika gently reached for her hands that were now shaking.

"Look at your wrists!" Her sister's eyes widened with shock as she took a closer look.

Deep purple abrasions wrapped around both of them. However, they lacked the pain one would expect from such wounds. The men's laughter echoed within her as the taste of a sweaty cloth in her mouth caused her to swallow hard.

"I was gagged," suddenly her memories were clearing. "But he saved me. How did he know I was in danger?"

"Who? Who saved you?" Her sister demanded.

"The soldier from the parade," Emel's eyes grew wide with excitement. "He brought me home and… I knew him. I knew his name. How could I know this?"

"What's his name?"

"I-I don't know anymore," Emel gazed out through the open window, the warming sun enveloping them.

"You're not making any sense now, Emel." Sidika sighed, peering at her as if she was possessed. "I told you there were evils roaming the streets. What if you were attacked by a Hortlak?"

"I doubt the undead are likely to leave anyone alive," Emel snapped, unable to control her irritation. "Anyway, you don't honestly believe in those things, do you?"

"You don't?"

"Of course not," she rolled her eyes. "They're as fictitious as the Ubir."

She bit her words back as another memory flooded her mind. She was in the arms of the solak, flying through the air. The familiar scent of tart blackberries with hints of ginger invading her nose and in that moment she remembered his name.

"Timur." She whispered. That was his name. The name of the soldier. The memories began flooding back to her as if they'd been locked away. The feelings Timur had produced within her, the touch of his skin, all of it rushed through her sending delightful shudders down her spine. The power of it made her head spin.

"What did you say?" Sidika looked up from inspecting Emel's wrists.

Emel suddenly felt strange divulging all of this to Sidika. If she told her sister that she remembered flying with Timur that night then she would likely run off and tell Manula. Or worse, their mother. Funda was even more superstitious than Manula and Sidika put together. She would make her walk around with a charm and knock on every piece of wood in the house if she found out. Which would take ages, not to mention she would be punished severely for once again breaking the rules. No, it was better for everyone if she kept her returning memories to herself.

"No," Emel finally replied.

"Emel," Sidika began, resting her hands on Emel's shoulders. "Promise me you won't go looking for this soldier again?"

Emel's heart flipped, unsure if she could make such a commitment. The hope of seeing Timur again filled her with unparalleled joy. She longed to be the focus of his expansive sorrel eyes, gazing upon her as if she were the only one he ever wanted to be around. She had never been as free as when she was with him. How could she live knowing she could never return to the very arms she had been searching for her whole life? Even if Timur was something more than human, it couldn't keep her away.

"Emel, you must promise me!"

"Fine, I promise I won't go looking." She silently hoped there was another way around this.

"Good." Sidika smiled, triumphantly crossing her arms. "Because if word got out about this it could ruin any chance of söz kesimi."

"What, have you heard something? Has the chief judge sent word to father?" Emel asked, suddenly sick to her stomach. Her heart thumped nervously in her chest at the prospect of this.

"I haven't heard anything specifically, just whisperings."

"Why didn't you say so before?" Emel exclaimed. "Tell me what you know!"

"When I got home last night Manula told me she thought she saw the chief judge come by the house only a few hours before."

Emel frowned. It was very unusual for father to take a meeting so late, especially with someone from work.

"You don't find that odd?" Emel asked.

"No," her sister replied. "I find it exciting. You could be married to Chief Judge Halil's son! Don't you understand what this means?"

"Yes, it means I will forever be related to the chief judge and his grotesque wife. Not to mention a slave to their son."

"You're being dramatic," Sidika rolled her eyes.

Fuming, Emel filled her lungs with a deep breath of air, taking a moment to calm herself. There was nothing more infuriating to her than when others tried to belittle her feelings.

"I'm not," she replied through gritted teeth.

"Fine." Sidika shrugged. "Maybe you're not, but you know he could one day become the grand vizier. You'd be set for life!"

"The only thing that would be set is my unhappiness."

"And what about mine?" Sidika raised an eyebrow. "Should you do anything foolish it could ruin my chances of being anything other than a concubine. Do you want that?"

"Of course not." Emel sighed, wishing things could be simpler for them.

It was common for girls who were not chosen as suitable mates to be pressured by their families into harems. Emel knew their family would be no exception should a scandal arise. This idea was worse than any arrangement. Yet, her mind continued to wander to Timur's piercing red eyes, glistening against deep olive skin. Her heart couldn't let go of him.

"Emel," Manula's voice urgently called from the doorway. "You're father sent me to fetch you. He requests your presence downstairs."

From the look on the maid's face, it was clear nothing good would come from meeting with her father. Catching her sister's meaningful glance, she knew Sidika was urging her to be cautious.

"Don't worry, Sidika," Emel whispered as she stood. "I'll be perfectly obedient."

With a new level of reluctance Emel had never experienced before, she followed Manula from the room. They rushed down the long hall belonging to her mother's wing of the house. The home was divided in two, one belonging to Funda and the other belonging to her father's second wife.

They emerged from the hallway, entering an enclosed balcony where Funda was often found enjoying the warmth of the tandir after a long bath. Manula continued to the staircase which was open to the sky above. The sun twinkled happily in comparison to Emel's mood that desperately prayed for the sky to open up and let its floodgates wash everything away.

"He's just beyond those doors," Manula instructed once they reached the main floor.

Emel's heart pounded against her chest and she was certain it would burst straight through her bones. Her hands were clammy as her nerves began to attack. Taking a step against her will, her feet moved seemingly on their own through the open door. The shutters were closed, leaving a dim haze to fill the room. At the far end of the room she saw her father, hunched over a row of papers. His slender hand, aged with time, was wrapped around a seasoned reed pen. Engrossed in his work, he didn't even take a moment to glance up as she sat down across from him.

Placing her hands at her side, she dug her fingers into the medlar brown cushion, its silky fibers nearly tearing under the pressuring. She sat there, studying his thinning face, accented by the wrinkles that scattered around his eyes and forehead. She willed his pursing lips to speak, but he continued to sit as if she wasn't there.

After an eternity, his narrowing eyes finally rose to meet hers. His nose wrinkled as if a putrid aroma reached him, but she knew it was his distaste of her presence. She could only imagine how much he'd hoped his first wife would birth a son, but instead he received nothing but girls from the desperate Funda.

"You are aware that you were visited by the wife of Chief Judge Halil, yes?" Her father's voice toneless and bored.

"Yes."

"Then you should already know that they were looking for a suitable wife for their eldest son, Hamid," Hasan-Ali continued, folding his hands firmly together.

She knew there would be no chance of debating her way out of this. Her father's determined expression conveyed the deal was already set. Her whole body shook as realization wrapped its persistent fingers around her heart. Terrified to move, she found herself paralyzed as her father congratulated her on her upcoming nuptials.

"The contract is being written as we speak," he concluded, his delighted smile taunting her.

"But—" She quickly clamped her mouth shut as anger flashed in his eyes.

"Understand this, child," his shrill voice swirling about the room. "You were not the chief's first choice. Their son is much too good for you, but as it stands there is more we can gain from this situation so I did what needed to be done."

The words stung and it took everything for Emel to keep the tears at bay.

"You can thank me now." He didn't have to voice the threat behind these words. He would sell her in a heartbeat.

"Thank you." Her chest tightened. Every part of her wanted to flip the table, to throw her father's precious papers in his face, but she had made a promise to Sidika. She would be obedient.

"The marriage festivities will begin soon, I'm sure the chief judge will want their son married before the end of the month."

She could only manage a nod as sobs threatened to overpower her composure at the thought of this. Her breathing quickened as sweat rose up from her glands. Panic was nearing and she desperately prayed for her father to excuse her.

"Very good." He smiled, triumphantly. "You may go. Rest well before kina gecesi."

Not able to stand another minute of it, she stormed from the room and into the outer sofa. She glanced around at the maids who were peacefully working as if the world wasn't coming to an end. Her mind raced with images of a life with Timur. A life where she could be free to be herself instead of a contractual obligation. That possibility was now gone. She should never have come home last night. Between her father and her sister's opinion of the arrangement, she knew she had no one else to turn to.

What if you searched for him? She asked herself, but wondered how she would be able to find Timur.

The palace was quite a lengthy walk from her home and even if she did get there she would not be granted entrance. Would he even be there? Or would she have to scour the barracks?

Stop it, she scolded herself as she cast the idea from her mind. There was no way that would end well for her.

With no other options, she wrapped her shawl around her head and made for the shore. If she was going to be prisoner for the rest of her life, she might as well enjoy the freedom of the ocean one last time. Her father might be able to give away her body, but her spirit would forever belong to the sea.

CHAPTER 8: The Conspiracy

The janissary barracks.

The next morning, Timur awoke even more puzzled than when he'd fallen asleep. From the sight of Queen Naz in the kizlar chief's arms and the bizarre episode of the sultan screaming about someone hurting his mother, he had too many questions. His thoughts turned to Emel, her beautiful golden brown hair curling down past her shoulders. Her eyes dancing in the moonlight. A smile touched his lips as the memory of Emel washed over him.

There were many things about this woman that enthralled him. It was frightening to feel so close to someone while knowing all the while that he would inevitably hurt her. This reinforced his confidence that he had made the right choice in removing her memory of him. By this time his compulsion should've removed him from her thoughts. His weakened state could've just delayed the effectiveness of it.

"Wake up," Adel's voice pulled him from his dreams.

The velvet, metallic scent of blood filled the room, reminding Timur of the hunger burning within him. It was always a surefire way to wake him up, but where was it coming from? The sun glistened through the open window, stinging Timur's eyes and making him regret ever opening them.

"Oof, someone looks unwell," his friend muttered, sticking his nose deep into the steaming cup in his hands. "I do love the smell of blood in the morning, don't you? It's a shame I can't have any until nightfall, but it cuts the edge."

Adel set the cup aside, crossing his arms as he leaned against the row of built-in cupboards they shared.

"Where'd you run off to last night?"

"Following a lead," he mumbled, finding it difficult to focus on their conversation while the blood taunted his need.

His stomach groaned for the cup, to drench his insides with its contents and live, but his heart ached for Emel. If only he could be in her presence, to feel the weight of his curse lifted from him again. But she would be forgetting about him soon, just as it should've always been. He'd allowed her to get too close, to see him for what he truly was and he kicked himself for putting her in that kind of danger.

"You met someone, didn't you?" Adel's question caught Timur off guard.

"What do you mean?"

"I can tell," he continued. "Her smell is all over you. What is that?"

Adel crinkled his bulbous nose, sniffing the air.

"Cherry with hints of—" He took another whiff and grinned. "Rose water. She must've been delicious."

Timur shook his head, certain he was still dreaming.

"Tell me." Adel crouched next to his mat, staring at him at eye level. "Where did you find such a delightful treat?"

"Stop it," Timur growled, his thumb absently reaching to the bottom of his forefinger to find that nothing was there.

Sitting up with a start, he realized it was missing. His ring filled with tutku flower. It was the only thing he had from before the janissary corp. From a normal childhood he would never remember. Pushing past Adel, he forced his aching body towards the cupboards.

"You did feed, didn't you?" The question hung in the air as Timur tried to find a way around it.

Flinging the nearest door open, Timur began emptying the contents of the cupboard. Panic set in, realizing he would surely break his fast if he didn't get his hands on the herb.

"Not again," Adel groaned, disapprovingly. "You know not feeding goes against everything you are, not to mention could kill you, right?"

Timur could barely hear Adel's scolding as his fearful heartbeat filled his eardrums.

"You may be the only Ubir I know who's had the gift since childhood, yet you're the weakest all at the same time." Adel was not helping Timur in the least. "You wouldn't be this weak if you drank enough blood to tide you over. You could even do that thing where you don't drink straight from the neck, yeah?"

Timur glared at Adel, forcing him to shut his mouth.

"It was just a suggestion," Adel rolled his eyes. "What are you looking for, anyway?"

"This." Timur sighed, pulling the ring from the back of the cupboard and kissing the top of the oval case.

The familiar abrasion of interlocking tulips stamped into the brass band felt like home against his fingers. Wrapping his fingernail around the release, he checked the contents of the locket. The pleasant aroma of berries with a hint of wet grass washed down his nostrils, overpowering the metallic notes that floated in the air. He closed his eyes, allowing the feeling to wash over him as he slid the ring onto his finger. The calm that filled his rumbling stomach was not as satisfying as the presence of Emel, but it would do.

"Would you like me to leave you and your trinket alone?" Adel chuckled.

The cabinet clanged shut as Timur rose to his feet, towering above Adel.

"It's tutku flower. It calms the thirst. You should try it sometime," Timur replied, walking out the door for morning prayer.

***

Adel shook his head in disapproval. He couldn't believe Timur could just let himself waste away. And for what? A principle that only applied to mankind? Adel pondered this question as he left their barracks, welcoming the morning breeze.

"Adel." The captain's voice came from behind him and he turned.

He did not expect to see the captain leaning against a nearby tree, its fan-shaped leaves provided enough coverage to allow Captain Yusuf to go unnoticed.

"Sir." Adel stood at attention.

"Rest easy." Captain Yusuf waved his formalities off. "Has Timur left already?"

Adel nodded as Yusuf motioned for him to follow.

"Is he feeding regularly?" The captain asked.

"Not lately," he replied, reluctantly. The captain would not like this news, but he wondered how long it would be before the captain abandoned Timur in his plans.

Adel looked over at the stocky captain, merely a few inches taller than himself. Frustration creased upon the older man's forehead.

"He must eat soon, otherwise he won't be ready."

"Why must he be involved at all?"

"He's the only one who can pull this off," the captain exclaimed, his eyes filled with passion.

The captain paused, taking a deep breath before continuing.

"Let's return to your barracks, there are things we must discuss in private."

Adel obediently followed the captain, his curiosity peaked.

"Now—" The captain turned to Adel once they were safely inside the small room. "I'm only telling you this because you have proven yourself trustworthy to the cause."

Adel's chest puffed at this revelation, barely able to conceal a smile.

"I know Timur is your friend," Yusuf replied, folding his arms as he began to pace. "This is why you've been tasked with keeping an eye on him. Yes?"

"Of course." Adel was unsure where the captain was going with this.

"Well, the reason the Eastern Faction relies on you to ensure Timur is getting stronger, the reason the whole plan was put into place is because it's been discovered who he truly is."

"Who he is, sir?" Adel asked, his eyes narrowing in confusion.

"He is the true son of the queen." The captain laughed in awe as if he were rediscovering this phenomenon for the first time.

"But… Sultan Mustafa is her son," Adel replied. "Last I checked she only had the one."

"I thought so, too." Captain Yusuf shrugged his shoulders. "But as it stands, Timur is her son."

"How do you know?"

"I have eyes and ears everywhere, you know this." The captain waved Adel's question off as if it was nothing. "As such, a weapon saturated with his blood, wielded by her kin is the only thing that can do what needs to done to ensure of Queen Naz's demise."

Yusuf spat at the mention of her name.

"This is why our past attempts failed." Adel's brow rose as realization set in. "If she is older than Timur, then it's possible that she's the first."

"Exactly."

"But if she's the first, how could she ever of had a Mustafa? He's human!"

"Now you're asking the questions we've been wondering since we first made this discovery." The captain rested his chin on the top of his fist, deep in thought as he continued treading circles into the plum-colored carpet.

"Either she's not the oldest and someone else is or—" Adel gasped. It couldn't be true. Could it? "Or the sultan is not her true son?"

"Precisely." A huge grin spread across the captain's face.

"Sir, if I may be so bold as to suggest, why don't we just tell Timur this. I'm sure the discovery that his own mother deserted him and has been standing in front of him this entire time would be enough to send any man to seek revenge. His loyalty will be ours."

"No," the captain replied, sternly. "We have to be certain this is what he would do. With as many questions as you say he's asked, he could want to be reunited for all we know."

Adel bit back the urge to argue with the captain. He knew Timur was curious about his past, but the virtue above all his principles was justice. He would never trust his mother after finding out who she was. Adel was certain if this.

"The discovery of Timur's mother aside, the plan is already set," Captain Yusuf said, slapping a hand on his slender shoulder. "You must get him to eat. Let him gain his strength. Then, during Eid al-Fitr, when the time is right we will force his hand. He will have no other option but to kill the queen."

***

Timur urged his frozen body to move away from the door. He had returned to fetch his prayer mat, but the sound of the captain speaking to Adel halted his advance. The captain's words rattled around in his mind repeatedly, making him unsure if he had heard them correctly.

"You must get Timur to eat... he will have no other option than to kill the queen."

His body went cold as these words repeated themselves in his mind. How could the captain be involved in such a horrendous plan? He couldn't believe this, let alone Adel would go along with it. And what was all this about them discovering who his mother was? For his friend to keep something like this from him was... unthinkable.

"Madness," he muttered to himself as he made his way to the front post to wash, deserting the idea of getting his mat.

He would just have to use the ones provided. It was not his first choice as the scent of human usually perfumed them, but it would have to do.

Washing his hands and feet, he attempted to scrub away his burning anger. The captain and his friend were working together to manipulate him. Whatever the plan was, it couldn't be good. And why were they so bent on him feeding? The more he thought about it the angrier he got.

As the prayer commenced, he attempted to set aside such thoughts to raise up meditations.

"Glorified be my God," the words began in repetition, but Timur could not concentrate.

The warmth rising up from the ground caused his thirst to flare as sweat dripped down his chest. His breath uneven, he could feel the heartbeats of the people around him. He felt the need to feed, but he had to endure. He couldn't let himself succumb to his desire. He shivered as the sound of blood pumping through the vein of a neck beside him grew even louder. Squeezing his eyes shut, he prayed for a cure to his disease.

A sigh of relief washed over Timur as the prayer came to an end. He rolled up his mat and left the presence of all the human soldiers as swiftly as he possibly could. For a moment he forgot about the captain and his plan to use Adel to get him to do their dirty work. But as soon as he left the front post it all came rushing back.

Storming from the janissary quarters, Timur decided he needed to take a walk to clear his mind. He didn't know what to do, but some fresh air might give him a new perspective. He looked about the vast city without truly seeing anything at all, his mind a blur of thoughts and questions.

How did the captain plan to force him into doing the very thing he swore he would never do? If Adel was relaying everything he said to the captain then surely he would've known this. Could he even trust Adel or call him a friend? They had known each other since they were kids, didn't Adel deserve the benefit of the doubt? But then Timur remembered the change. Adel becoming an Ubir. Had it changed him? Or had it just enhanced what nature was already there?

Every other blood-drinker he knew remembered being turned, they remembered who they were before. Timur had none of these luxuries. Or curses, depending on who was asked. He couldn't help but think about what he could've been like as a human. Perhaps he was worse than as an Ubir. He often thought this might be the case. After all, there were only two kinds of monsters in the world. The ones who craved blood and the ones who didn't.

"Watch where you're going!" A man shouted. Timur looked up from his feet in time to see his scowling face.

"Sorry—" he stopped when a woman emerged from the crowd behind the man, escorted by her maid.

His heart skipped a beat as the familiar feeling of humanity returned, removing the thirst for blood. It was her. It had to be her. He pushed through the bustling street, needing to remove all distance between them.

"Emel!"

The maid glared at him from behind her shrouded face, guiding her charge farther away from him.

"Please, wait!" He quickened his pace.

"Why is he staring at us?" He heard Sidika ask.

"Come on, Sidika," Manula whispered, ignoring her question as her free hand grasped the locket about her neck. "We best be on our way back now."

Stopping in his tracts, his heart fell when he heard the name. It wasn't Emel after all, but her sister. Sniffing the air, Timur recognized the scent of tutku flower. Their faces may have been covered, but he knew exactly who they were. But how was it possible that even Emel's sister had the gift of suppressing the Ubirdi thirst?

He pondered this as he watched them leave, the ache in the pit of his stomach returning. He welcomed it this time, for what was the point in feeling human if he couldn't enjoy it with the one woman he cared for? There was no replacement. No substitute.

Shaking these thoughts from his mind, he returned to his walk. His insides rumbled and he begged his mind for a distraction. The sight of Adel conspiring with the captain flashed before him once more, his anger returning with a vengeance. How could his only friend betray him like this? It didn't make any sense to him. He knew he would have to confront Adel at one point, but he couldn't decide where to start. He didn't know if he was more upset with Adel for plotting to manipulate him into killing the queen or for keeping the knowledge of his mother from him. He swallowed the painful screams that threatened to burst forth from him. He wouldn't give Adel the satisfaction.

The sigh of waves crashing over rocks onto the shore brought Timur's attention to his surroundings. He'd been so deep in thought he hadn't bothered to watch where he was going. He stood at the brink of a cliff. Gazing out into the vast blue-green ocean, he watched as the surf lapped up onto the cove's beach below. A smile crept upon his lips and the wind blew through his chin-length hair. He welcomed it, taking in a refreshing breath. Delightful scents of sea foam and salt met his nose. The cawing of seagulls swallowed the distant sounds of the bustling city behind him.

A scream startled Timur from the moment of tranquility he'd found.

He scanned the beach, using Ubirdi power to see past the surface of the shimmering water. Below him, a head was bobbing just above the surface. Looking down at the steep and jagged descent to the bank, he wondered if he had enough strength to make the jump. Another cry and a loud splash pushed him over the edge, propelling his body through the air.

Managing to move his legs directly underneath his body, he glided closer to the ground and prepared to land. As he landed, a rock sliced through the bottom of his foot. He braced himself on the cliff wall to inspect. Dark maroon-black paste seeped from his skin, but he would live. Hopefully.

Returning his focus to the water, he spotted the body and dashed into the ocean's depths.

CHAPTER 9: A Body in the Water

Along the Bosporus waterway.

The water lapped at Timur's clothes as he moved towards the floating body. He was soon waist deep and pushed his toes into the rocky floor, ignoring the tingling of saltwater on his injury. His self-healing was slowing, a sign that his body was decaying. He'd gone several days without feeding, but he couldn't bring himself to break his fast. Each time he was tempted his heart ached for another way. Another day with Emel, but he prayed for her sake that he'd never see her again.

With eyes opened, he dove into the salty waters and swam up to the form. In one swift movement he wrapped his arm around the body and began moving towards the shore.

"What are you doing?" The body cried just as he felt a foot kick him.

He looked down and was surprised to see Emel attempting to squirm from his grip, her captivating blue and gold irises sparkling up at him. His empty stomach was full again, his fangs no longer throbbed, but most importantly his heart was whole. A lightness filled his body and the distress he was filled with before was washed away by her.

"Timur?" She asked, blinking the water from her eyelashes.

"How… how do you know my name?" He asked, dumbfounded.

"You told me." She grinned. "Would you mind letting me down?"

"Oh, of course." He swiftly let go of her waist, gently setting her back on her feet.

Timur couldn't wrap his head around how she could still know him. His attempt at washing her memory of him definitely did not work.

"Are you okay?" He asked, concern etched across his brow.

"Yes, why do you ask?"

"I heard a scream and you were floating in the water…" he trailed off, mesmerized by her beauty and the power her presence had over him.

"I didn't know anyone else was here so I thought I'd go for a swim. Then something in the water brushed up against my leg." She blushed, sending his heart soaring. "Must've just been some seaweed."

"Come," he said, pulling her into his arms. "Let's get you to shore."

"It's like reliving last night all over again." She winked, wrapping her arms around his neck.

Timur's heart skipped a beat and he desperately wanted to embrace Emel forever. But he had to force these desires aside. He could never let himself be with a human and she had to forget about him.

"Why so quiet?" Her fearless voice taunted the reservation in his heart.

Setting her down on a smooth stone next to the bank, he thought about how to respond. He had to be careful, he had already allowed himself to get too close to her before. He couldn't make this situation worse.

"I'm just surprised to see you here." He smiled.

As Timur took a seat next to Emel, he noticed that she was once again without a veil. Or the turban she'd been wearing during the night feast. Her hair was loose, laying in golden brown, soaked waves over her shoulders. Beads of saltwater dripped from her Grecian nose onto her lips. Lips the color of ripe hünnap berries in the spring. Her wet tunic clung to her body, drawing his eyes down the form of her leg to her feet. Her toes were curling into the warmth of the rocky sand as she looked out towards the sea. She was oblivious to the feelings she was stirring within him. She looked up at him and smiled, the light dancing around her irises, and he quickly looked away. His heart thumping at being caught.

"Isn't it beautiful?" She sighed, resting her smooth palm against the stone they sat on.

She was at ease, even though she was in the presence of a dangerous beast. How could she be so calm? So lovely?

"Look at how the wind picks up the buds from the Erguvan tree." Her voice was just above a whisper, drawing him closer to her with each breath. "I love seeing the wisps of violet flying through the air. Free. Unencumbered by the weight of this city. Don't you?"

"I've never noticed," he replied, looking around at the snowfall of purple flowers. Most of them fell into the ocean, their freedom short lived as the tide washed them back onto the shore.

It reminded him of his attempts at ridding himself of the Ubirdi life. Each time Adel was there to force him back from the brink of death. Was it because he was a friend? Or because Adel was just following orders from the captain? He wasn't certain if it even mattered. Either way, he was sure he would need to confront Adel sooner rather than later.

"You're bleeding!" Emel exclaimed, peering down at his knobby feet.

"It's nothing." He shrugged.

He moved his foot away from her view, but it was too late. Her eyes were shocked as she saw the tissue was slowly stitching itself back together.

"Incredible." Her face awash with wonderment. "You can heal yourself, too?"

His eyebrows furrowed at the mention of *too*. She wasn't supposed to remember that he had healed her wounds.

He gazed down at her wrists and a stab of guilt flooded him that soon turned to rage. There were still bruises where the traders had tied ropes around them. They should've been gone by now. He should've been strong enough to prevent this from happening to her.

"I'm sorry," he whispered.

"For?"

He nodded towards her wrists.

"You didn't do this," she replied. "You actually healed them, though with a few side effects."

"There weren't supposed to be any side effects." He retorted before he could think through his words.

"Do side effects not normally happen when Ubir heal others?" She asked.

"You aren't supposed to know that."

"Why not?" She asked, her expression revealing she knew more than what was good for her. "Because you did something with your eyes that meddled with my memory?"

Her fingers brushed a few stray curls from her kingfisher eyes that perfectly captured the sun.

"And yet you still don't fear me? Even though you remember what I am?"

"What you are doesn't matter to me, it's what you do."

The conviction in her words moved him. The trust in her voice, the adventure in her eyes and the fearlessness her heart exuded made her irresistible. But she was too innocent to the ways of the Ubir. She had never witnessed one feeding and she had no idea that he had once attempted to take some of her blood. The thought of it made him grieve. He was detestable and didn't deserve to even be in her presence.

"So what brings you out here?" She asked, unaware of the somber thoughts running through his mind.

Filled with uncertainty, he looked at her.

"It's okay, you can always try that memory erasing thing again." She laughed at her joke, the music of it filling Timur's heart with joy.

Her eyes lit up as a small, crooked smile crawled upon his lips.

"I used to come here with a friend when I was young," he admitted. "It was our secret fort. A hideaway from our responsibilities to the janissary corp."

"You've been a soldier for a long time, haven't you?"

He gave a single nod. "My entire life."

"And what happened to your friend?" She asked.

"He's a solak as well." He paused for a moment. "Though, I'm not sure he's still a friend."

"Why not?"

A deep sigh escaped him, conveying his distress.

"When he became an Ubir, he took to it like a moth to a flame," he began. "It changed him. Made him greedy for…

for what sustains us. I didn't notice it at first, but the frequency has increased. That, and I caught him speaking behind my back with the captain. They are planning something and whatever it is involves using me!"

He realized he was shouting and stopped, resting his head in his hands. Her warm hand rested on his back, rubbing in circles to soothe him.

"Perhaps it's not what you think," she replied, causing him to peek out from behind his hiding place.

He raised his eyebrow, not sure what to make of her retort.

"I overheard them speaking in our barracks," he explained. "They discovered who my mother is and didn't tell me. The captain is also having Adel spy on me and to get me to eat so that I'm strong enough to do their dirty work."

"Are you certain? Is that all that was said?"

Timur admitted he'd only heard the end of their exchange, but the captain's last words were clear enough.

"You don't know who your mother is?"

He shook his head. "I was abandoned at a janissary training camp as a child. I never knew by who. This—" He looked down at the ring on his right forefinger drawing Emel's attention. "Is all I have from the past."

"And you don't remember anything else?"

"No."

"Why aren't you eating?" She continued her interrogation.

He realized he had shared too much. He should've anticipated this question would come. The concern on her face pulled at his heart, he didn't want her to worry about him. Yet, she had no idea what sustained him. If she did he knew that she would run in fear. Perhaps this was for the best, though. He needed some way of keeping space between them.

"Because, I'm an Ubir," he finally replied. "For as long as I can remember I have never been human. I eat as you do, but it doesn't keep me alive."

"What keeps you alive, then?" He heard her heart skip a beat, the lovely melody distracting him.

It wasn't the reaction he was expecting. Her daring heart sang in what he could only describe as joyous anticipation. Curling his lips over his teeth, he hesitated. Once he took this leap there was a chance he would never return. Revealing himself to her was already breaking about a dozen laws and for it the Ubir community would surely imprison him. But how would they know if he had or not? Despite being risk averse, he decided to take the plunge.

"For years I've vowed to never kill for food as other Ubir often do," he said, turning away from Emel. "In the past I've only taken a little, just enough to stay alive. But I hate how it makes me feel."

He paused, looking down at Emel who sat next to him. A tinge of guilt struck him. She didn't deserve to know that such evil existed.

"So where is it?"

"Where's what?" He was taken aback by her abrupt question, but thankful for the distraction. Perhaps she would forget about asking what he ate.

"Your tail, of course. I've heard the stories of the Ubir."

His eyes widened and a deep chuckled bubbled up from within him.

"My what?" He asked in between bouts of laughter.

She giggled along with him, both enjoying the sound of it bouncing between the rocks.

"From the stories, the Ubir always had a tail," she explained. "Come to think of it they also had giant heads, but yours is quite average. I mean, not that your face is average, it's extraordinary. It's the handsomest face I've ever seen."

Pink speckled her cheeks as she bit her lip. To think this brave woman could ever be shy enough to blush astounded him.

"Thankfully the stories are just that." He winked, for once feeling at ease.

"My sister says such lovely things about the Ubir." She rolled her eyes. "I never believed in them, but she did."

"I actually ran into your sister and your maid, Manula, just before I arrived here," he replied.

"Probably searching for me."

"When I saw them I thought it was you for a moment."

"Really?" She grinned. "Were you disappointed?"

"Very." He chuckled. "But why would they be searching for you?"

She grimaced, returning her gaze to the crashing waves. Wringing her hands, it appeared to Timur that she was rather nervous.

"What is it?"

"I may have snuck out without permission." She shrugged.

"May have?" He raised an eyebrow.

Turning back to him, her guilty smile gave everything away.

"I did." She laughed, the heartwarming tune filling the air.

Her rebellious nature both taunted and amused him. If only he could be as spontaneous, as brave.

"I'm actually happy the Ubir are real," she said.

"You're happy about it?" He couldn't have heard her right.

"Yes, of course I'm happy. Without you and your abilities I would be..." She bit back the tears he sensed were rising.

Taking a deep breath, she continued. "I've always thought that if Ubir did exist, most humans wouldn't understand what they were. They'd probably just demonize them, which they have."

"They aren't wrong," he said just above a whisper, looking down into the vastness of his empty hands.

"They must be," she whispered, swiftly placing her hand in his, stringing her fingers through the laces of his own. "It must be a lonely world for you."

His hands held onto hers like his life depended on it.

"You haven't said it out loud, though I suspect I already know." A lump formed in his throat as Emel pushed for the answers he resisted to supply. "But I need to hear it. What do you eat?" She looked expectantly up at him, searching him. He couldn't take it anymore.

Letting her hands fall from his, he desperately wanted to tear the skin from his own body for what he was. Studying her determined expression, he knew he wouldn't be able to get out of this one. Taking a deep breath, he silently begged for her forgiveness.

"Blood." He winced as he vocalized the word.

"So why haven't you taken mine?" She asked.

"Sweet Emel—" his voice broke, unable to control the pain. "Believe me, from the moment I saw you, the craving left me. The need for blood vanishes when I'm with you."

Her eyes were deep in thought and his heart wanted to leap from his chest. It was a mistake to reveal himself to her. He should never have let his guard down that night when he discovered that she was the köçek. Yet, if he hadn't she would have been taken by those horrible men. He couldn't have allowed that to happen, not to his Emel.

She's not yours, he reminded himself, shaking the thought from his mind.

"But you'll die." Her voice was filled with sorrow when she said this.

"It is for the best."

Her eyes narrowed in anger and she stood up, clenching her fists.

"But you're not a monster!" The fury in her voice startled a nearby seagull into the air. "You say that there are others who kill for their food, but for some reason you don't. You're different. You saved me! Who will be here to save us from the other Ubir when you're gone?"

He rose to his feet, wanting to calm her, but his head spun at the sudden movement. His heart expanded and shook, his lungs pulling in quick spasms.

"Timur?" Emel's voice was distant.

His vision blurred, and he fell to his knees. Arms wrapped around him, shaking him to wake, but the darkness was stronger. It seeped in like water rushing into a sinking ship and soon there was nothing.

CHAPTER 10: Dead Man

Emel raced to Timur's side as he fell to the ground. His lips turned gray and his hands shook as a coldness crawled from the center of his heart, spreading to the rest of his body.

"Timur!" She cried, but she knew he couldn't hear her.

Had he gone too long without feeding? She couldn't let him die. He had saved her life and showed her the freedom she had always desired. She needed him.

Kneeling beside his limp body, she rested his still head upon her lap. She scanned the soil around her, searching the rocks for one she could use. A pinkish rock with white jagged edges caught her attention among a pile at her side. Reaching for it, she pulled up her tunic sleeve.

She took a final deep breath, filling her lungs with bravery. She could do this. She needed to do this. Without another thought she placed the sharp end of the rock at the top of her wrist. Pushing into the surface of her skin, she dragged the rock across her forearm. A painful cry filled the air. Her eyes watered as the bright red blood seeped from her self-inflicted wound.

"Please." Tears poured from her eyes as she parted his lips, bringing her wounded arm close to him.

She carefully guided her blood into his mouth.

"Come back to me!" She cried.

Timur's cold hand latched onto her arm, pulling her wound deeper into his mouth. She closed her eyes, biting back a whimper as his sharp teeth threatened to puncture her skin.

Timur's eyes flew open, his irises flashed crimson as he pushed himself away from her.

"What have you done?" He gasped, wolf-like fangs protruding from either side of his gums.

"You were dying," Emel replied, defensively.

"You have no idea what kind of danger you put yourself in!" Timur leaped to his feet, turning to walk away.

Emel's cheeks flushed, rage filling her. Hadn't she just saved his life? Shouldn't he be grateful for such a sacrifice? She rose from the dirt, standing proudly as she cradled her wounded arm.

"You're welcome," she said, her chin rising.

Timur turned, his eyes softening at the sight of her laceration.

"Here, let me heal you." He offered, but she pulled her arm away.

"Why would I be in danger for saving you?" She asked.

"You won't let this go, will you?"

She shook her head.

"Let me heal you, and after I'll tell you."

"Tell me first and then you can heal me." She negotiated, determined to have answers.

"Fine." He ran a strong hand through his messy hair before continuing. "I'm different than the other Ubir. Not only because of my choices or because I can't remember ever being human, but also because I can turn humans."

"What?" Emel gasped, unsure if she heard him correctly.

"My fangs, they're... they're poisonous. This is why I never eat directly from the source." He replied. "If I bit you, I could've turned you into an Ubir."

She saw the pain this brought in his eyes and her heart ached for him.

"If I turned you," he whispered, stepping closer to her. "I fear it would remove this."

He rested his large hand upon her heart.

"Your humanity," he whispered. "Your fearless, bold, and pure humanity. You were right the other night when you said you had a power."

"What would that be?" She asked, searching his eyes as they dissolved back to their normal sorrel hue.

Her nervous heart thumped with anticipation at his touch.

He smiled. "Like I said, you take my thirst away. And you've captured my heart."

"Then why do you run from me?"

He reached for her hand and in one motion her question was answered. He wrapped his other hand over her wound and she felt the energy from his palm radiate over her. The fibers of her skin stitching themselves together before she could even blink.

"You are fearless, loving, and quick to trust. All things I am not. I would only ruin you. Which is why you have to forget about me."

His words stung as she prayed they wouldn't come to pass.

"Shouldn't I get a say in all this?" She asked, not wanting to meet his gaze.

"Please don't make this harder than it already is." The palms of his hands wrapped around her cheeks, gently raising her head. His eyes filled hers, revealing the passion behind his hesitation.

"Don't leave me again and I won't have to," she whispered.

Without another word, is hands moved around her shoulders, brushing his fingertips down the sides of her arms before tangling themselves into hers. His gaze moved to her lips as he pulled her into his iron chest. Electric shivers ran down Emel's spine when he met her parting lips. Energy escaped him, through his mouth into hers. It filled her heart, sending butterflies into her chest.

His hand snuck around her waist and lifted her up into the air. She pulled away from his lips as a fit of laughter escaped hers. Her heart was at peace as he danced in circles on the beach with her in his arms.

***

Grand Vizier Zaganos treaded lightly among the rows of records kept by the nishanji. His heart threatened to escape his chest as he knew he shouldn't be there. Remaining in the shadows, Zaganos searched for anything related to the decree made by Queen Naz to expand the borders. The Eastern Faction would be waiting for a report and he knew he couldn't return to Captain Yusuf empty handed.

Remembering his failed attempt to keep the janissary troops from going on campaign, he was motivated now more than ever to ensure the decree went missing. He knew he would be executed on the spot if he were caught, but if he didn't do exactly what was asked of him they would take his family. Everyone knew what it meant to lose their human family to the Ubir. It wouldn't be just for food, it would be for entertainment as well. He'd witnessed this first hand after he'd been promoted and turned. This couldn't happen. Not to his beautiful Persian wife, Maryam. His whole heart. No. He would do as Captain Yusuf asked, even if it meant putting himself in danger of Queen Naz herself.

"There you are," he muttered to himself, his shaky fingers curling around a large, recently inscribed scroll. The authorization to release Captain Yusuf's unit to the borders of Hungary signed by Sultan Mehmed, in his scratchy forced penmanship, and Nishanji Hasan-Ali lay in his hands.

A rustling breeze jolted Zaganos from the parchment. He scanned the room through narrowed eyes, the chamber seemingly still. Movement from above caught his attention and he surveyed the painted glass windows which lined the ceiling. A few birds fluttered here and there, but otherwise there was no movement from behind the outer walls.

Satisfied that he was alone, he rolled the scroll back up and pocketed it in his robe. He checked to ensure he was leaving the nishanji's desk exactly the way he'd found it. A row of reed pens lay in a meticulous fashion next to a stack of fresh paper. It was clean, tidy, and undisturbed.

The soft footsteps on the stone pathway outside alerted him that he had stayed there much too long. Bracing himself for departure, he turned and nearly ran into a body that stood too close for comfort.

"Oh—" His voice shook, startled by finding that he wasn't alone after all. "Didn't realize you were there. So sorry."

Without even looking up to see who the man was, he turned to leave only to have a large fist grab him, turning him around.

"What are you doing here?" A gruff, but familiar voice asked.

"I-I… was just searching for… for something." He rolled his eyes at himself, frustrated he'd not prepared a better excuse for such an occasion as this. But the grand vizier hadn't planned on being seen at all. An oversight he wished he hadn't made.

He looked up into the confused eyes of Chief Judge Halil and puffed a sigh of indignation. The judge clearly wasn't supposed to be there either.

"I could ask you the same thing." He chuckled, his eyes darting towards the exit.

"I was sent here by Nishanji Hasan-Ali." Halil scoffed. "As for you, I know you're not supposed to be in here."

"Ah well." Zaganos shrugged with a chuckle, his white beard bristling. "I was on my way out so if you'd be so kind."

He eyed the chief judge's wrinkled yet firm grip that remained on his shoulder hoping this would be the end of their confrontation.

The chief judge huffed, but regretfully complied.

"I will see you in the morning." Zaganos waved his goodbye as he turned to leave.

"Wait."

Only managing to distance himself a few steps, he froze. Closing his eyes, he prayed the chief judge would just let him be. With hesitation, he turned back to face the towering form of Chief Judge Halil.

"Yes, judge?" Zaganos replied with reluctance.

"I think you may have dropped something."

His eyes followed the chief judge's which were locked upon a scroll that was rolling from underneath his fur-trimmed robe.

I keep meaning to ask Maryam to fix that pocket, he thought to himself, cursing his forgetful nature. His devoted Maryam was the only one who could put up with it.

His eyes grew as the chief judge rounded the corner of the nishanji's desk. Zaganos recognized the look of anger in the chief judge's eyes.

"Allow me to assist." Halil sneered through his graying moustache and recently shaved chin. It was a look Zaganos hardly understood. He couldn't trust a man without a beard.

Chief Judge Halil bent at the waist, scooping the parchment into a fist. The judge never once took his eyes from the grand vizier. He probably thought if he did that Zaganos would take that chance to run away. He wouldn't be wrong, either.

"What could this be," the judge asked, raising a bushy eyebrow as he slowly unrolled the parchment.

Zaganos' heart raced as fear wrapped its greedy paws around his entire body.

"It's nothing," he croaked. "Just some reminders for myself. You know me, always forgetting something."

He lunged for the parchment before the judge could read the lettering, but the taller man yanked it from his reach.

"We both know this is so much more than a to-do list." The judge scowled, scanning over the decree.

"Oh well, my mistake." Zaganos shrugged. "Must've picked it up by accident. They all look the same."

The two men stood there, locked in a threatening stare down unsure of what would happen next. The chief judge was the first to move, his long stride removing the space between them.

"Traitor," the judge growled, his fangs protruding.

"No-no-no, you've got this all wrong," Zaganos whimpered. He knew even in his fully fed state he was no match for the chief judge. His power was much greater. Zaganos wrung his hands, his claws beginning to puncture through the cuticles.

The chief looked at the grand vizier's claws in mock pity.

"Those won't help you now," The judge hissed, his fingers grabbing Zaganos' jaw.

The judge lowered his gaze, his eyes flashing crimson as they bore into Zagano's fearful ones.

"I've always known you were weak, but I never imagined you to be disloyal to the empire."

"Please, don't do this!" He cried, his eyes weeping. "They will take my wife and children, I had no—"

Halil punched the grand vizier in the gut, knocking the air from him.

"This is why you're unfit for the title you hold! So easily manipulated." Halil's fingers moved, wrapping around the grand vizier's loose neck.

Zaganos gasped as the judge's hold tightened. Using his entire strength, he tried to get out of Halil's grasp to no avail.

"Please!" He gulped, his lungs begging for air.

Securing his grip around Zagano's neck, the chief judge reached for his belt, brandishing his mech. Halil's expression twisted into a look of death as he began stabbing the grand vizier repeatedly in the chest.

"You would stop the nishanji and me from succeeding in removing you." Halil's voice faded as Zaganos' vision blurred. "It is better this way… Hamid will make a much better grand vizier…"

These were the last words heard by Grand Vizier Zaganos as his Ubirdi body fought for air one last time.

CHAPTER 11: The Danger in Hope

Outside the nishanji's home.

"Is there anything I can say that would make you stay?" Emel asked, her eyes watering at the idea of them parting ways forever.

Timur gazed down at her, his eyes filled with love and sorrow. He placed his palm against her cheek, taking her breath away.

"Don't," she whispered, clutching his hand. "I don't want to forget."

"And I don't want you to." Timur shuddered when she touched her palm against his calloused knuckles.

"Then stay," she pleaded.

Hesitation emanated from his entire body and Emel sensed he was pulling away. Wrapping her fingers around his neck, she pulled herself closer to his firm body.

"You're right." She chuckled. "My parents would never approve."

The corner of his lip perked up in a half smile.

An idea suddenly struck her, filling her with hope.

"We can run away, Timur. Just you and me. Then we would never have to part."

"Emel—" he began, but her lips quickly silenced him.

When they parted, his brow was creased as if struggling with how to respond to her proposition.

"Whatever your captain is planning..." she whispered in his ear. "It's not for your benefit. But together, we can go away and never look back. We could leave all this behind us."

Timur shook beneath her grasp and she knew he had made his decision.

"There isn't enough tutku flower in the world that would convince me I wouldn't one day hurt you."

"I know you won't." She caressed his angular jaw, welcoming the aroma of amber that emanated from him.

"Please?" She prodded. "I can't bear to be without you."

Timur sighed. "But where would we go?"

"Anywhere." Her spontaneous heart roared. "We could travel east across the Ottoman lake, or west to the Aegean Sea!"

"Not west," he growled through clenched teeth.

She wondered what was so bad about going west, but she kept these thoughts to herself.

"Okay, not west then." She shrugged. "But you agree?"

"This isn't a good idea, Emel," he murmured, resting his hands on her shoulders. "We don't have anywhere to go."

Emel pondered upon this for a mere moment before an idea sparked.

"Then we go to Chios."

Timur's eyes narrowed as if he had never heard anything more baffling.

"Chios? What's there?"

"Manula still has relatives there. I could return as her. They wouldn't know the difference."

"And what about me?" His brow rose with doubt.

"What about you? You won't need to worry, you have the ability to change people's memories."

"I can't just compel everyone." He laughed.

"So that's what you call it." She smiled. "You won't need to compel everyone. Just the ones who suspect you as an Ottoman warrior."

"This is crazy." He shook his head.

"It's crazy not to try and be together," she countered. "We could build a life there. Manula has told me so much about the small island I feel like I've already been there."

His chiseled chest heaved with a defeated sigh.

"How can I deny you?"

Emel squealed with excitement, her whole body floating on air as she imagined the life they would enjoy.

"I'll first need to confront Adel," he confessed.

"Of course."

"Once I have the answers I seek I'll return."

"How long will you be?" She asked.

"With my new energy running through my veins I'm sure I'll manage to squeeze the truth out of Adel in no time."

Emel grinned, knowing he was referring to the blood she had gifted him.

"I will return tomorrow after nightfall." He promised.

"I'll be waiting for you at my window. It will be the only one open, facing the back."

She pulled Timur in one final kiss before the looming night forced them to part ways.

***

The mesmerizing bouquet of cherry and rose water followed Timur as he left the nishanji's home. Emel's breath still lingered upon his ear, her joyous confidence in her plan pulling at his heartstrings. She was much too hopeful that this would work. He couldn't imagine a future without being with her, but was this even possible?

You will get her killed, his better judgment warned him, but he shook this idea off.

He had, regretfully, made a promise to Emel. They would leave together the next nightfall. He wouldn't waste another moment pondering this choice. He had other matters to attend to.

Pivoting, he directed his pace towards the palace. Adel would be nearing the end of his rotation outside of the sultan's chamber. An opportune moment to catch him off guard. It would be harder for Adel to lie if he didn't expect him.

The familiar sound of a blade being unsheathed whispered through the trees that framed the main entrance of the palace. The sound stopped Timur in his tracks, his muscles tensing as each hair on his forearm stood up. Something was dreadfully wrong. Sprinting through the front gate, the sound of this boots clattered against the stone path. Scanning the main courtyard, he saw the ordinary guards strolling about the garden. The scent of their humanity made his nostrils flare, but he had no time to entertain such thoughts.

"It is better this way…" a voice was saying and he followed the direction it came from. "Hamid will make a much better grand vizier…"

Whose voice is that? He wondered. It was familiar, but he was having trouble placing it. Whoever it belonged to, there was something not right about it.

As he raced down the long corridors that framed the garden, he wondered why there weren't any Ubir present among the soldiers to hear this. There should've been at least a lieutenant among them, but his senses told him the closest Ubir was the one he'd just heard.

Pushing himself through gold embellished doors, he entered the still record room. He could barely see anything in the dim light, but the aroma of blood flooded his senses. The acidic nature of it could only belong to that of an Ubir. Someone had killed an official. But who could it be? It couldn't be Emel's father, could it? This was, after all, where the nishanji's office was.

His eyes adjusted as he crept his way further into the chamber. A breeze fluttered the loose sleeves of his tunic and his left hand went to draw his bow. His fingers searched his back, but they returned empty. He hadn't bothered to stop by the barracks before coming to interrogate Adel. How could he have known there would be any reason to?

Reaching to his belt, he sighed with relief. At least he had remembered his mech. Grabbing the silver handle of the short sword, he smiled as the steel sang in the air. Taking careful, yet purposeful steps, he glided like a bat through the darkness.

The body came into view just as a sliver of light shone down from a window in the intricately painted dome ceiling above. The man's eyes were frozen wide with tears of blood running from the corners. His mouth lay gaping, still and without life. Timur noticed deep bruises covering the old man's neck, revealing he'd been strangled. But what finally took the Ubir's life was a knife to the heart, the weapon in question lying at Timur's feat. The evidence of the dead man's human past began to reappear across his porcelain figure. An old facial scar crawled from his right cheek down to his lip, his Ubirdi claws retracted and returned to their prior form. All the signs of his Ubirdi durability vanished making him nearly unrecognizable.

Nevertheless, Timur knew exactly who this dead man was. From all the times he'd attended the queen's meetings, he knew each one of the council members. He could tell who they were in a crowd of thousands. The man who lay dead, murdered before him was none other than Zaganos, the grand vizier.

Scrolls lay strewn across the nishanji's desk, rolling onto the floor. There had been a struggle.

But why would the nishanji do this? He wondered.

Feet shuffled in the darkness and he saw a dark shadow fleeing towards the doors.

"Who's there?"

The form did not heed his call and quickly disappeared. Running from the council room, Timur scanned the pathway, but no one was there. A whistle echoed through the air and within minutes two high ranking soldiers were marching towards him.

"Allah'a şükür!" Timur sighed with relief, waving them down. "Someone has murdered Grand Vizier Zaganos."

The soldiers sniffed the air, their fangs flaring at the aroma that warned an Ubir had been killed. They eyed Timur suspiciously, their gaze falling upon his weapon. He quickly sheathed his mech.

"I didn't do this," he said, lifting his hands in defense.

"Give us the knife," the lieutenant ordered, his eyes flashing crimson as he pinned Timur against the ornate wall.

"Let go" He growled, locking his eyes on the lieutenant as he pulled from the reservoirs of his Ubir strength to compel his captor.

"That won't work," the lieutenant sneered through sharp fangs. "I can smell you're half fed. Weak."

"Hey, isn't he that solak who starves himself?"

"I think you might be right, Nebi." The man chuckled a throaty hiss that made Timur's skin crawl. "He's the imposter."

"Didn't he say something about someone being dead in there?" the Ubir named Nebi asked. "Should I go check it out?"

The lieutenant nodded his approval as the soldier disappeared behind the chamber door.

"I promise," Timur said, trying to reason with the lieutenant who glared at him. "I had nothing to do with this. I was on my way to relieve a solak from his duties when the scent reached me. I came to help, but he was already dead."

The lieutenant didn't budge, as if Timur hadn't spoken.

"There was another voice I recognized," he tried again. "He said something about someone named Hamid being a better fit?"

"Sir," Nebi's uneasy voice called from the doorway. "The grand vizier's dead… murdered."

The lieutenant's cold eyes reeled back to Timur who shifted in a helpless attempt to pry himself from the man's iron grip.

"Let's take him to The Gate," the lieutenant commanded.

Timur's thoughts raced as Nebi pushed him from the palace towards the walls that surrounded the city. The grand vizier was dead. In the nishanji's office, no less. Who was that man who spoke just before he walked into the chamber? Was it, indeed, Emel's father? Or someone trying to kill him, but found the grand vizier by mistake. Whoever it was must've been the true murderer. But how would anyone believe him? There were no other witnesses.

They trudged down the dark path, the lieutenant taking every opportunity to trip Timur. Stopping in front of the fortified walls, the lieutenant unlocked a barred gate leading them into the prison hall lined with cell doors.

"Here's where you'll rot." The lieutenant chortled through his scraggly beard as he opened the nearest cell.

He reeked of rotten flesh.

Timur's jaw clenched, biting back the urge to attack. Not wanting to be accused of another crime, he had to think before allowing his pride to flare.

His body lurched forward as he was kicked into the empty cell, his fingers catching his fall as they curled into the rocky surface. He pulled his large frame from the ground, his head skimming the top of the stone ceiling. Wrapping his hands around the steel bars, he peered out from the darkness of the cell.

The sound of the ocean lapping against the rocks met his ears, reminding him of Emel. The memory of the day they had shared made the corners of his lips turn upward.

"Find something funny?" Nebi asked, knocking his fists provocatively against the door.

Timur glared at the man through bared teeth, but the soldier was hardly disturbed. His crimson eyes narrowed in return with a strength that mocked Timur.

"I am innocent," he growled, rage rising up from the depths of his cold heart.

"Yeah, yeah, that's what they all say." Nebi cackled, his body too close for comfort.

His breath quickened as he seized the moment, grabbing the soldier's collar as he yanked him against the cell door.

"You will regret this." He promised, spitting in his ear.

A sharp pain ignited like fire through his side, propelling him back against the slime-covered rocks. He reached for his side, his eyes widening when his hands returned dark, foul-smelling blood. The lieutenant rattled the tip of Timur's blade between the bars, a drip of Timur's blood falling from it echoing throughout the prison.

"Lovely weapon." The lieutenant's upper lip curled, peering down at Timur's wound. "I think I'll keep it."

The two Ubir soldiers chortled as they made their way towards The Gate entrance, locking him in the darkness.

The silence of the cell surrounded him, leaving chills down his arm. Removing his tunic, he used it as bandage around the gash in his side. Applying pressure, he tried to make himself comfortable, knowing it would be awhile before the janissary agha would see him. But would he be able to get to Emel's window by the following nightfall? His eyebrows furrowed as doubt quenched whatever hope Emel had instilled within him.

His heart ached at the thought of her waiting for him, not knowing that it wasn't for a lack of desire but that he'd been mistakenly imprisoned. A fury rose from the pit of his stomach as his fangs punctured through his gums. He had to find a way out. No matter the cost.

CHAPTER 12: Betrayal

The janissary barracks.

Adel's chest heaved as he darted between the rows of wood-framed buildings which housed the janissaries. Spotting his destination at the end of the alley, he flung his entire body into a full sprint towards the doorway. He didn't even bother knocking before bounding into the room.

Captain Yusuf, seated on a dusty cushion on the floor, looked up from the parchment in his hands. A lamp illuminated the windowless space and the air was thick like the shutters hadn't been open in some time.

"He's been taken," he gasped, his breath uneven after running for so long.

The captain made no attempt to help the distraught soldier as he waited for Adel to explain.

"Timur, they found him outside of the nishanji's record office." The words fell from his mouth faster than he could contemplate them. "The grand vizier's dead and they're holding Timur responsible."

The captain swore, slamming the parchment down causing the short table to rattle uneasily.

"Where is he now?" The captain barked.

"A cell within The Gate. I followed them as soon as I heard. It's not far."

"Then why didn't you stop them before they even got to him?"

"I-I was still on shift." Adel was unable to meet the captain's gaze that was blazing holes into his skull.

"You were given a direct order," Captain Yusuf huffed. "And in the end you ignore it for a duty that doesn't even matter? The sultan means nothing to the Ubir!"

Adel bowed his head low.

"It's okay," Yusuf said, folding his arms. "Lucky for you I'm adaptable."

He peered up at the captain from beneath heavy eyelids.

"Tell him what you know of the queen and what she has done to us. There's no need to mention that she's his true mother, of course." The captain grinned. "And since you say he has a soft spot for the humans, lead him to believe we will make it a better place for them. I will speak to the agha to release Timur. But only if he agrees to take the queen out. Tomorrow. After sunset."

"But sir, we aren't prepared for—"

The captain raised his hand, silencing Adel's protest. Captain Yusuf's decision was final.

***

A cell within the outer gate.

Plunk... plop... splash...

The sounds of seawater dripping on the rocks assaulted Timur's ears as he fought the sleep that loomed near. Exhausted from being up all night trying to pry his way to freedom, Timur's hope of making it out in time to meet Emel was dwindling. Why did he have to go and follow that voice? If he'd just followed his plan he wouldn't be in this mess.

A cool breeze howled through the dingy corridor as the scent of an Ubir tickled his nose.

Pushing himself from the rocky floor, he peered out from the reinforced bars.

"I know you're there," Timur cried out.

"Good," a familiar voice whispered from the shadows. "At least you're alive."

Adel's short frame came into view and Timur growled.

"Whoa, easy there." Adel's hands flew up in defense. "I've come to offer you a way out of this mess."

"I heard you and the captain," he retorted, ignoring the carrot Adel tried to dangle before him.

The surprise in Adel's eyes satisfied Timur.

"Tell me." Timur's voice was just above a whisper, but filled with the intensity of a desperate man. "Who is my true mother?"

"I can't tell you that," Adel replied. "Not yet."

Timur's fists shook the bars, the sound echoing about the damp walls.

"How could you keep something like this from me?" He demanded. "All the times I confided in you and you lied to me."

"I never lied to you." Adel shook his head. "I only just found out."

"Then why won't you tell me?"

"The captain has forbidden it," he explained. "But if you agree to do us a favor, I'll tell you everything once you've succeeded."

"And why would I agree to this?"

"You do want out from this hell hole, yes?"

The thought of Emel waiting for him made him rethink his approach to Adel. Perhaps there was a chance he would make it in time to meet Emel.

"What would you have me do?" Timur asked, hoping it wasn't what he suspected.

"Take Queen Naz out. Tonight."

Timur was hoping he wouldn't say this.

"You know the vow I took," Timur replied, his voice filled with desperate sorrow. "I will only take a life when we are at war."

"We *are* at war!" Adel hissed. "Why can't you see this? We've been the queen's puppets for too long. You even said she shouldn't be in power. It is our time to rise up from beneath the ashes."

"Why me?"

"Because you're the only one who can do this," Adel replied. "When fed, I mean *really* fed, you're the only one of us with enough strength to take her down."

"I won't kill her," Timur growled.

"If you knew what I know about her you might rethink that."

Timur's eyebrow arched. "What am I missing here?"

Adel sighed, resting his shoulder against Timur's cell door.

"I didn't want to have to tell you this, but…" Adel paused, as if unsure where to begin. "You have to promise me you'll keep this to yourself, okay?"

Timur rolled his eyes, but nodded his agreement.

"Not many know this, but the captain and I used to live in the same village. We didn't know each other, but he knew of me. He also knew Naz before she bequeathed herself with the title queen over the Ubir."

Timur's ears perked, not knowing there'd ever been a time before Queen Naz was there leader. Perhaps it was during a time when he was human, if he'd ever been one.

"I never knew the full story until I was turned, then the captain revealed the truth." Adel's voice quivered for a moment, quickly clearing his throat before continuing. "Do you know why I've never told you how I came to the janissary camp?"

Timur shook his head.

"My family was taken from me. Killed by a band of Crimean Tatars. Like wolves they destroyed everything." Adel's eyes grew distant as if he were reliving that very moment. "It's lucky I was very good at hiding, finding a space under the stairs. But I saw everything."

Adel wiped his lips with the palm of his hand before looking up at his old friend. Timur had never heard this story before. He couldn't believe they had been friends for so long not knowing this pain lay behind Adel's boastful exterior.

"Naz was the leader of this band. The captain says these were her first Ubir minions." Adel's voice fell in volume, as if there was anyone close enough to overhear him. "That day my family wasn't her only victim. They swarmed Captain Yusuf's home. Queen Naz herself dragged his wife and children out into the streets and slaughtered them. That's the last memory the captain has of being human."

Adel stopped, looking down at his hands as his claws punctured through his cuticles. Taking deep, calculated breaths he slowed his anger.

"I had no idea." Timur didn't know what else to say.

Despite the feeling he had of there being more to Adel's story, he hated witnessing his friend this way. Perhaps Emel was right, maybe he didn't have a choice in keeping his mother's identity a secret from him. For now he would give Adel this benefit of the doubt, but he wouldn't hold his breath.

"Timur, my brother." Adel begged as he reached into his robe and removed a large jug. "Naz has destroyed everything and she will soon destroy the empire if we don't stop her."

From the luscious aroma that wafted through his nostrils Timur knew that it was filled with blood.

"Think of the humans Queen Naz plans to enslave." Timur's eyes couldn't move from the container, unable to resist. Every inch of his body was drawn to its contents.

Adel brought the container closer. "Do this with us. With me."

A shiver ran through his body as his fangs threatened to break through. He desperately needed out, to be with Emel. If it was only this one task that could reunite him with his cure, is love, his forever, then it wouldn't be so bad. He was certain he could return to his fast before the obsession seeped in and took control.

A vision of broken bodies lying, mangled, all around him, blood pooling at his feet sent him cringing into the furthest corner from the blood-filled jug.

"No!" he cried, remembering why he had made the vow.

"Timur, I'm not asking you to drink from anyone's neck. I understand you don't want to turn anyone."

Adel knelt down, his eyes peering into the dark cell.

"I only ask that you return to your full strength to take down Queen Naz."

He watched in horror as Adel slipped his hand through the bars, bringing the jug within his reach. Closing his eyes, Emel was all he could think about. Her wondrous eyes sparkling in the light, matched only by the contagiousness of her smile.

"I can't be without you…" her majestic lips spoke to him, pleaded with him.

Timur couldn't contain himself any longer. His eyes flew open and ripped the jug from Adel's fingers, devouring its contents.

Crimson veins crawled down the length of his arms. Every fiber in his muscles tore, growing larger with each contraction. Black spikes jetted out from deep under his skin, replacing his fingernails with large claws. The constant gnawing of starvation was replaced by a fullness. But the fullness was artificial, a replacement for what he truly longed for. When the mission was over, he would return to her.

Wiping his lips on the back of his wrist, he threw the empty container at Adel's feet.

"So… do we have a deal, Timur?"

"Yes."

"Then I shall return once the arrangements have been made for your release," Adel smiled. "We shall attack at nightfall."

***

Emel awoke to the gentle tune of a tree sparrow. Rubbing sleep from her eyes, she opened the shutters and welcomed the brisk morning light. The bird greeted her from its perch on a cypress that loomed nearby and a warm smile tingled her lips.

Today would be the start of a whole new life. The thought of Timur by her side made her heart flutter to the beat of the sparrow's chorus. She could see their beautiful life together. A little house on the sandy shore, surrounded by the ocean. Timur would come back from a long, but pleasant day of fishing and she would sell them in the market.

Her stomach rumbled at the thought of food and she regretfully left her daydream behind in the room. When she reached the landing of the first floor, a swarm of servants flew by. Their words were hushed and quick, carrying crates filled with spices and jewels.

"What's going on, Manula?" She asked when she spotted her walking by with her hands wrapped around a large bowl of tulips.

"Haven't you heard?" she asked, her eyebrows jetting up in surprise. "Tonight is your Kına Gecesi ceremony."

"WHAT?" she cried.

Manula set the flowers down and embraced Emel.

"How can this be? I didn't even know there was a marriage date set!"

"It's okay," Manula whispered, rubbing soothing circles across her back. Something that normally would bring Emel comfort. This time it didn't help.

Livid blood pumped through her as she thought about why her mother would keep such a thing to herself. Pushing Manula aside, she stormed back up the stairs to the balcony where she knew Funda would be.

"How can Gelin Alma be tomorrow? The wedding day never happens so soon!" Emel's voice rang through the open floor, scaring a flock of birds from the branches that curled around the open windows lining the balcony.

Funda didn't bother to move from her perch, taking up the length of the sofa on the far end of the room.

"You're lucky there's even a wedding at all," she murmured, her hazy eyes far away.

"What do you mean?"

Emel took a step back as Funda's livid eyes locked on hers. "After what Sidika told us, it's a miracle there's still an arrangement."

"What did she tell you?" Emel asked, fearing the worst.

"You've been sneaking out again. Sidika saw you with a man last night. She's says that it's not the first time you've met him."

Emel's heart sank. How could her sister betray her like this?

"Thanks be to God your father was able to convince the chief judge to move up the ceremonies."

Chills ran down her arm as she realized this would be her last chance to run away. Her mind raced with all of the complications this created for her plans. Would Timur come before the festivities began?

"The women will be here tonight, you must get ready."

Her stomach churned at the thought of being married to Hamid. She'd never met the boy, but she knew he would never live up to Timur. Good thing they would be long gone by morning.

"Yes, mother," she replied, not wanting to set off any alarms.

Funda raised an eyebrow, but made no further comment as Emel headed for her bedroom. Her mother was right, there was much she had to prepare for, but the Henna Night was not one of them.

CHAPTER 13: Kına Gecesi

Nishanji Hasan-Ali's home.

Emel sat on the windowsill, gazing out at the setting sun. Her heart beat nervously as she waited in anticipation for the night to come. The few things she needed were packed and tucked away from any unwanted scrutiny, but still accessible if she needed to leave in a hurry.

Her heart longed for Timur like it'd been an eternity since she'd seen him last. She wondered if he was feeling the same way.

A timid rapping noise came from the door, pulling her from her thoughts.

"I don't need anything, Manula," Emel called, hoping to be left alone until the very last minute.

She needed to be gone before the night's festivities began.

"Emel?" Her sister's quiet voice came from behind the closed door.

The mere sound of Sidika's presence forced her posture rigid. She was the last person Emel wanted to speak to. She would try to make some sort of excuse or reason for why she told their parents about Timur, but Emel didn't want to hear any of it. There was no excuse for such a devastating betrayal.

"Go away," Emel called after another knock came from the door.

"Let me explain."

Letting out a puff of air, Emel turned from the window and marched over to the door. She swung it open just as her sister was about to knock again.

Motioning her sister into the room without so much as making eye contact, she returned to her window seat.

"Please, make yourself at home," Emel muttered through gritted teeth.

"Thank you," her sister replied, not getting the hint.

She took several careful strides before turning to face Emel.

"Emel," she began, taking a deep breath as if it would help build her courage. "I'm sorry that I hurt you, but you gave me no other choice. After I saw you return with that soldier last night? What if he had never brought you back?"

"What if I wasn't planning on it," Emel retorted under her breath.

"What was that?" Sidika asked, raising an eyebrow.

"How could you tell them?" Emel cried, ignoring her sister's patronizing question. She didn't have to answer to Sidika. She was the older sister, after all. Her eyes returned to the empty road. It wound its way across the length of their home and disappeared just beyond the border of their home.

Her eyes searched for Timur, hoping any minute he would make is way around the row of Persian silk trees that lined the street.

"You promised me you wouldn't go looking for this man again! That you were going to follow the rules, be obedient, and instead you're risking everything! And I know you were with him again yesterday."

Sidika's shouts echoed throughout the room, threatening to alert the whole house. She wished her sister would use more discretion.

"I had to tell them." Her sister concluded. "It was a matter of safety."

"Of safety?" she asked, whirling back to face Sidika.

Emel's nostrils flared, her fists balling up causing her sister to flinch. She was certain this was the biggest fight they'd ever had.

"The only unsafe part in this whole scenario was trusting you," Emel hissed, her words flying faster than she could process them.

Closing her mouth, she immediately regretted her words that clearly cut deep wounds within Sidika. But her sister had betrayed her, sharing privileged information she thought she could trust her own sister with. She would have to learn sooner rather than later that there were consequences for such an offense.

"I don't want to lose you—" Sidika's voice broke as tears swelled in her eyes. "But I'd rather you never speak to me again and be alive than dead."

Emel watched in silence as her sister wiped at the tears that were now spilling over like a waterfall. Swallowing hard, she knew she should go to Sidika and apologize. Her heart longed to embrace her sister, but pride latched its greedy hooks around her wrists tethering her to her perch at the window.

"I'm sorry it had to be this way," Sidika whispered before pushing her unsteady feet towards the door.

Emel didn't stop her. Her sister thought she was doing the right thing, but she was wrong. Sidika hadn't seen the chief judge's wife. She had no idea what kind of hell was waiting for anyone in a marriage to that family.

The sun hung low in the sky and soon the night shrugged its way in, casting shadows through Emel's open window. Each shuffle in the dark, every whistle of wind that fluttered through the leaves made her heart leap with hope only to be disappointed. Timur was still not there and her room was beginning to feel much too crowded.

"Where should I put this rug?" Manula's voice asked.

"Roll it up and exchange it with this one," Evranaki responded, but Emel hardly glanced in their direction. "All these colors must change before Funda enters."

Where could he be? Emel wondered. Her ears heard everything that was going on around her, but her mind was too distracted to process any of it.

The door swung open and she jumped. The humming of chatter floated through the open space, filling the room. Funda entered just as Evranaki and Manula were removing the last bit of green from the room. Funda's squared face was set in an emotionless line, examining everything until she was satisfied that the room was clean. God forbid there be any traces of green to be seen.

"It's time." That was all Funda said before throngs of women piled into the room.

Aunts, grandmothers, and cousins swarmed in and soon Emel couldn't even see the back wall. Her eyes darted back to the window, but still Timur had not arrived. Fear gripped her as she realized they had run out of time.

She couldn't understand what would make him so late. Had he been lying to her this whole time? Was he only pretending to need time to get answers so that he could get her out of his way? Hot tears filled to the brim of her eyelids, remembering the way his steel hands had held her gently in his arms. The sweet scent of amber and musk that radiated from his caramel skin was still pungent and she begged herself to forget.

She must've sounded so stupid suggesting that they run away. Why couldn't his compulsion work on her? She wanted nothing more than for her memories to be pulled from her.

"Sweet Emel." The memory of Timur's words as they sat near the sea wrapped around Emel's body like a warm blanket. *"You've captured my heart."*

Chills ran down her arm as her heart began to float. He couldn't have been lying about his feelings for her. She'd felt it herself and the look in his eyes told her his words were true.

He'll be here, Emel silently sighed with relief.

"Ahem." Funda cleared her throat, gaining Emel's attention.

Her eyes bore into Emel like knives as her face twisted into a disapproving scowl. She motioned for her daughter to stand in the center of the room. It took all of Emel's self-control to keep from rolling her eyes as she obediently took her place.

"We must get you ready for the ceremony." Funda feigned a smile as Evranaki delivered a long robe made of velvet.

The dark plum fabric had gold threaded tulips that cascaded from the shoulders down to the bottom hem. The weight of the robe made her sweat as her eyes kept darting towards the window. Had something bad happened to him? Had her father caught Timur before he could reach her? These thoughts plagued her mind as her mother retrieved a small, ornately decorated box. Evranaki quickly removed the lid from the box Funda held, revealing the black, clay-like contents.

"Close your eyes," Funda ordered.

Emel reluctantly obeyed, her mind racing at the thought of Timur being in trouble. It would explain his not showing up. But what could she do?

She jumped at the touch of Funda's fingers smearing the cold paste onto her eyelids and brows. Her eyelashes stuck together at odd angles as she opened them. She snuck her hand up to fix them, but her mother slapped it away.

"Don't touch."

Huffing, Emel returned her hand to her side as her mother picked up a red veil. Funda ceremoniously draped the fabric over her daughter's face as one of the women in her family began to play a rhythmic drumbeat. She couldn't tell who it was as there were too many relatives blocking her view.

She was led from her room and down the stairs to the main sofa, followed by all of the women in her family line. When the procession reached the main floor, the view of her future husband's family emerged filling the entire opposite side of the room. She could make out the large form of her future mother-in-law standing towards the front with a large roll of silk in her hands. She cringed at the thought of the chief judge's wife being her mother and having to live in her home.

The plumpish woman placed the silk she held onto the floor and unrolled the fabric creating a direct path between them. Candles were handed among Emel's family and lit.

"Go!" Funda hissed in Emel's ear, motioning for her to walk down the silk.

It was the only thing between her and the groom's mother. Her mother-to-be.

Maybe it won't be that bad, she thought to herself.

But when she saw the malicious grin upon the woman's face she was reminded of what this woman had said during her evaluation.

"My Hamid likes a girl with more meat on her…" A shiver ran down Emel's spine at the thought of being married to anything that came from this woman.

What if she never saw Timur again? What if she was about to enter a marriage with a man who would never love her for anything more than her childbearing hips? She had to find a way to escape before dawn.

A push from her mother reminded her she hadn't moved. With one last breath, she took a step down the path laid out before her. As she made her way down the aisle, the rest of the women in her family followed beside her. A few women began tossing small coins in the air, letting them scatter over her head. It was supposed to symbolize fertility, but for Emel it only brought a headache to torment her temples.

When she reached the end of the cloth, she stood before her future mother. Taking her mother-to-be's extended hands, Emel reluctantly kissed them. The room filled with the melodious sounds of women raising their voices together in song.

Sorrow clung to Emel's soul as the women sang of the separation that would occur in the morning. Each word emphasized that she would be leaving everything she ever knew.

"Is she crying, yet?" A woman's voice whispered in between verses. "Not yet, but she will need to. This one needs all the luck she can get."

She fought the tears these women prodded for. Blinking away the moisture that rose up and threatened to spill over. She would not give them the satisfaction. Even if she cried all of the tears in the world, it wouldn't bring this marriage enough luck. It could only bring her sorrow and an empty heart longing for more.

Timur's sorrel eyes that flickered crimson filled her mind and a tear escaped her as the realization that she would never see him again set in. None of the women seemed to notice as they ushered her onto a cushion on the floor. A cold numbness filled body her as coins were forced into her open palms.

She kicked herself for not insisting on going with Timur when she had the chance as defeat clung to her very soul. What if her family never left her side until morning? What if she never had another opportunity to run away?

"Do you want to know why you're being married to Hamid?" the chief judge's wife asked in a low voice as she painted Emel's fingers with henna.

The pudgy woman didn't wait for a response before continuing. "Because your father is the only one who can promote my son to grand vizier. So know this, you will never mean more than a contract to my Hamid."

The woman's words seeped through to Emel's heart, burning it from the inside out. As her chest heaved with sobs, the women around her celebrated her sorrow. Everyone danced in delight as the unmarried women had their hands painted in the hopes of being married next. Emel's stomach churned at the sickening sight of the excited girls looking upon her with envy. They had no idea the doom that awaited her marriage.

I have to escape! She thought to herself, repeating the words in her mind like a soothing lullaby.

CHAPTER 14: Treason

The Palace.

The stars sparkled high in the sky as hundreds of footsteps whispered against the flagstone. The silhouettes of the Eastern Faction swarmed the palace like ants covering every entrance.

With his mech drawn, Timur followed alongside Adel and the other men as they raced up to the main gate.

"Halt!" A guard stepped out from the darkness, but was soon silenced by Adel's quick reflexes.

The blade slicing through flesh competed to be heard against the cicadas that plagued the night air. The guard's eyes rolled back and the body flopped over onto the stone.

"Too bad we have no time for a snack," Adel muttered as he stepped over the lifeless form.

Timur froze, a shiver running down his spine as his eyes locked onto the decadence gushing from the slitted throat. Human blood perfumed the air. It called to him with all its metallic glory, beckoning him to sink his teeth into the luscious fat.

The idea made him question why he'd given up the practice in the first place. The raw power that ran through his veins at the mere taste… the sensation of his fangs sinking gums deep into the vein…

"Glad to see you still got it in you." Adel grinned back at Timur.

"What?" Startled from his reverie, Timur met the knowing glance of his friend before he disappeared through the front gate. "No! I don't know what you're talking about."

Cursing himself for being tempted, he glanced around to be sure no one else was watching before he stepped over the fallen body. He pushed to keep up with Adel, scanning the dim courtyard for the covered archway they were instructed to enter. Scattered cypress trees loomed over the landscape, breaking the light shining down from the full moon.

Sweat dripped from his brow, its salty tang reminding him of the precious moment shared with Emel in the Bosporus waters. It seemed ages ago. If he wanted any chance of returning to her he had to stay alert. And clean. He couldn't risk being high on blood. Who knew what he would do to her then? He couldn't even fathom picturing it in his mind.

The promise of being in her calming presence, basking in her golden blue gaze urged him forward.

Adel motioned for him to stay close, ducking behind a pillar which framed the path before them. It was just as Captain Yusuf described.

His heart thumped in his ears as they searched the hallway. Adel's eyes flashed crimson, adjusting to allow his vision to see through the darkness. Timur followed suit.

"There." Adel pointed towards a staircase at the end of the hall, one leading downwards and the other going up.

"You go up, I'll go down?"

"Did the captain say to take the first staircase to the upper level?" Timur asked, eying Adel warily. He was always prone to breaking from the plan.

"Come on." His friend chuckled, knowing exactly what Timur was thinking. "Where's your sense of adventure?"

Probably with Emel, he thought to himself. But he didn't dare share this.

"Go, then." He growled, heaving his body up the stairs taking them two at a time.

The steps ended at a passageway. Scanning the place, he found there was only one spot that would give him the best vantage point of the eunuch's courtyard. His veins pumped, flooding his body with energy as every molecule vibrated. Even now he could feel his power waning, crying out for him to refuel, but he couldn't give in to their request. Drinking more blood would surely result in him killing someone, or worse turning them. No, he would have to press on.

Lunging, he hurled himself through the air. Guiding his body upward, he landed atop the roof of the tower with ease. Peering across the dark expanse, the whitewashed rooftops glowed in the night. Between the domes lay a dark gap, rectangular in shape. It was the opening to the eunuch's courtyard, the location where the soldiers were now working to corner the queen.

Stepping to the ledge of the rooftop, he peered down into the courtyard. There was no sign of life, but he could feel the air tightening as the queen's presence made itself known. He could sense her prowling in the rooms below.

Sniffing the air, the subtle notes of the other soldiers surrounding the queen were barely discernible. They had drenched themselves in tutku flower oil, allowing the aroma to mute their natural Ubir scent. It was a smart tactic as now they could take out anyone who did not smell of the herb.

Crouching near the ledge, he peered into the night, drawing his bow as he prepared for his mark.

***

Queen Naz stormed through the palace with an anger so great it made the war brewing in the west look weak. Her Ubir soldiers hadn't shown up at their usual meeting and she couldn't sense any of them in the stillness of the palace. There was something in the air that was familiar, a scent she couldn't quite put her finger on. It misted through the inky night leaving a haze wherever she went. She needed to find Bayar.

Surely he'll know what the hell is going on here, she thought to herself.

Rushing into the eunuchs quarters, a chill ran down her spine at the sight. Bodies blanketed the floor, their eyes still and lifeless.

"BAYAR!" She bellowed into the ether.

Her deep-set eyes narrowed as a shadow slipped around the corner. Sniffing the air, the peculiar fragrance grew stronger and clearer. Although she couldn't identify the main aroma, she recognized its undertones. They belonged to an Ubir, but whatever they'd perfumed their bodies with muted their essence.

Clever, she mused, a sneer spreading across her angular face. *But it won't be enough.*

Her eyes shifted, bright red flashing from her irises as they illuminated the passageway. She sauntered around the lifeless bodies as she followed the direction the shadow had fled.

"I know you're there." She sang, her head tilting to one side as she peered around the corner.

Much to her dissatisfaction, the shadow was not there. Moonlight glittered from a stained glass window overhead, illuminating the long, bloody hall that stretched out towards the courtyard of the eunuch's. Stepping over a limp arm, she knew the only exit from here was through the courtyard.

A shuffling came from behind her. Whirling around, she was once again met with nothing but the lifeless eunuchs sprawled upon the floor. She was just thankful she did not see Bayar in the mix of it all.

"Call for your queen," a harsh voice floated to her ear, causing her sharp, black claws to extend through her cuticles. "Cry out for her and your life might be spared."

Spinning on her heel, she raced for the courtyard entrance. Shadows danced about the golden pillars that lined the whitewashed floor as she emerged from the palace. At the center of it all stood the kizlar chief, a knife to his throat. The man wielding the weapon was of a stocky frame, dressed in uniform. His face remained in the shadows, but it was evident that he belonged to the janissary.

"Ah, if it isn't the honorable valide sultan." The soldier's ruby eyes floated in the darkness. "I've been waiting for you."

"Let him go," she ordered, the power in her voice shaking the earth below her.

A cackle drenched with arrogance echoed between the tiled walls.

"You're strong, but it won't work on me," the soldier taunted.

Heat rushed to her cheeks. Why didn't her command work? Ubir were harder to compel, but she was always able to muster enough energy to bend their will to hers.

The shadow's chuckle hit a nerve with Naz. Her nostrils flared as a darkness filled her body.

"I said, let. Him. GO!" she snarled, the walls cracking under the pressure of her compulsion.

The order bounced off of the soldier once again and he remained as though she had said nothing.

"Oooh, that tickled." The soldier shrugged, tightening his grip on Bayar.

Naz forced herself to be still, her eyes locked on the blade that was pressed against the kizlar chief's neck.

"Your compulsion won't work on me, not while I'm on this blood."

The soldier pushed the kizlar chief forward, stepping into the light. A smooth, graying beard covered a diamond shaped face plagued with lines. Though he had aged, it was a face she would know anywhere.

"You've done well for yourself, Captain Yusuf." She cocked an eyebrow. "But I never took you for a traitor. Why do you do this, after all I've given you?"

"You've given me nothing," he snarled, tightening his grip on the eunuch.

Her eyes warned Bayar not to move as Yusuf's knife threatened to plunge through his collar. She had a plan.

"You forget." She chuckled, folding her long, clawed fingers in front of her. "It was you who came to me."

She smiled, satisfied when he made no response.

"You were just a simple lad," she cooed, taking a careful step forward. "Son of a leventis, doomed to follow in his father's footsteps. I only gave you what you asked for. A life of purpose and prosperity."

"At least I could've been happy as a naval soldier!" The Captain puffed his chest out with pride. "But you were sure to remove any chance of that."

"There's no need to get upset." Her words pulled upon her power as she raised her hands in defense. Her eyes flashed crimson, but it made no difference. Her power was useless against the captain.

"Tell me, who's blood are you on that can withstand my power?"

"I think we both know whose blood this is." The captain smirked.

"I'm sure I don't."

"Well, only consuming the blood from your veins would provide enough power, but I'm sure you wouldn't leave yours just lying around."

"Of course not." She sighed, her patience growing thin.

"Only a few know you have a son."

"Everyone knows I have a son." She chuckled, amused by such a statement. "That's the only reason I'm valide sultan."

The kizlar chief's fingers itched to move, but Naz flashed him a warning look.

"Not the sultan, but an Ubirdi son," the captain clarified.

"That's not possible." She scoffed.

"That's what I thought, too," the captain agreed. "Until I met him."

Her eyes darted to Bayar, hoping it wasn't true. Yes, she'd had a child but Bayar was supposed to make sure this was never known. The kizlar chief's eyes widened and he gave a subtle shake of his head. He hadn't told a soul, but if it wasn't him then who else could've known?

"How long did you think this could be kept a secret?" The captain continued to prod. "A child with Ubirdi power, never having been human before. Such strength is abnormal even as an Ubir. But I found him."

The captain's chest puffed up with pride.

"And what do you suppose on doing now, holding him for ransom?" Her pearly white fangs sparkled with greedy anticipation. She would enjoy killing the captain. "I left him as a baby and never thought of him since. Do you really think that's your best move?"

The captain erupted in laughter, making her skin crawl.

"Hold him for ransom?" His grip loosened on the blade. "Don't be absurd. I know better than to think you sentimental. No, I have spent my life building up my own empire. My own followers who see what you truly are. A monster."

"Oh lovely, I see why leventis are a curse to Constantinople," she spat, glaring at the traitor before her. "It's time to put the dog down."

In one swift movement, Bayar grabbed the captain's wrist, yanking the blade away from his neck as he spun himself under his attacker's arm. He shoved the captain's own knife into the man's thigh before taking it. An ear-splitting cry filled the air as Bayar pulled the weapon out, dark blood oozing from the wound.

"That's better." Naz grinned as Yusuf fell to his knees. "Tell me, where can I find my *other* son?"

"You'll never know," the captain replied just as Bayar's fist slammed into his jaw.

Walking to his side, she looked down at the broken captain, crumpled at the feet of Bayar. "I'll only ask it once."

Yusuf spat at her foot in reply.

"Kill him," she ordered.

Bayar's eyes gleamed with approval as he raised the blade to finish the job. As his arm swung, a man lunged out from the shadows and grasped Bayar's fist. The force of the impact sent the knife clattering to the ground. Bayar grunted as he yanked himself free, turning towards the intruder.

As the two men fought, Naz's eyes darted towards the captain as he struggled to reach for the fallen weapon. She sprinted in his direction, scooping the knife up just before he could get his hands on it.

Propelling her body forward, she leapt through the air towards the wounded captain, sending the knife deep into the captain's shoulder. His blood-curdling cry piercing the night air.

"Perhaps killing you would be a mercy," she growled, the veins in her neck pulsating, like worms, underneath her milky skin.

"Watch out!" Bayar's strained voice warned her as he dropped the dead body of his attacker.

She whirled around just as an arrow flew from behind one of the nearby archways. Her hand shot out, snatching the arrow's shaft inches from hitting her square in the face. Another arrow shot out and she ducked, letting the arrow whiz by. She heard Bayar's muffled cry as the bolt made contact. The soldier set his bow aside and charged for her, wielding a blood drenched sword aimed straight for her heart.

"NO!" a cry echoed from the rooftops above as the queen used the solak's momentum, forcing the arrow she held deep into his flesh.

Eyes wide, the young solak stumbled back. His hands grasped for his chest as his whole body turned stark.

"This is what happens when you follow the command of a leventis." She glared into the dying man's eyes.

"Now," the solak gasped, glancing up towards the stars as thick Ubirdi blood dripped from his lip onto his unkempt beard. "Do it now, my brother."

His body fell in a heap before her, his pearly skin turning dull as his human scars and imperfections returned. She followed the solak's gaze up to the courtyard's opening above.

"I know you're there!" She called into the night air. "Reveal yourself!"

CHAPTER 15: Gelin Alma

Timur's heart pounded in his ears as he peered down at Adel's body. This wasn't a part of the plan. No one was supposed to die except for the queen. But the queen wasn't supposed to be his birth mother. His fingers itched to unleash the arrow from his bow, but he couldn't bring himself to pull the trigger. It was as if he were seeing the queen for the very first time. She was the one who had left him all those years ago, the one whose blood ran through his veins. The thought of it paralyzed him. He knew his duty to the captain, to Adel, and to his country would be to let go of the string. To let the arrow plunge into her heart. But what about his duty as a son?

Peering over the ledge, he froze as he met the queen's gaze.

"Come on down," she whispered, gently.

Swallowing hard, he flung his body over the ledge. His feet were barely audible as they landed on the stone floor.

He winced as his hand scraped the harsh surface, stinging the cut on his palm that hadn't yet healed. He now understood why the captain needed to lace the arrows with his blood. Footsteps of the captain's soldiers as they fought off the rest of the men loyal to the queen echoed on either side of the courtyard. She had nowhere to run. Rising to his feet, he drew his bow once more, aiming it directly at her.

Chills ran down the length of his arms as her wicked eyes flashed crimson. It was just his luck that his birth mother would be the one woman he loathed most.

"Kill her!" The captain gasped, his breathing labored as his body tried to stitch itself together around the knife still deep within its tissue.

"What's it to be, my son?" She asked, her dark eyebrow cocked.

The image of Sultan Mustafa cowering frantically at the feet of Queen Naz flashed before his eyes.

"No, no, don't take me to her!" The sultan had shouted. *"Don't take me to her, I beg you!"*

Timur blinked as the memory faded. He was suddenly filled with clarity.

"You've been compelling him to believe you're his mother his whole life." Timur studied her reaction carefully.

"My dear boy." Queen Naz tilted her head to one side, a pout upon her lips. "Put that silly thing down. We have much to catch up on, after all these years."

"Don't move," he ordered, adjusting his hold on the bow's string.

"You think your command will hold me?" She laughed wickedly, taking a step closer. "I'm your mother, deary."

"But you're not the sultan's mother, are you?" Timur growled, ignoring the queen.

She took a step back, but each retreat he matched, keeping her in his line of sight.

"That night he was crying out for his mother, but when he was in your presence he begged to not be taken to you!"

"Well, you know how kids will be." She chuckled.

"You're the reason his mother is dead!" Anger rose up from every inch of Timur's body. "And you're the reason I have this... this curse!"

"This curse?" She scoffed. "What we have is a gift. A gift I have fought to preserve. I was born to a world veiled from humanity, ruled by a corrupt Assembly who thought it best for those with this gift to be slaughtered. But I escaped into the world of mankind where we are not only equals, but rulers, And it's because of me that this empire stands as mighty as it is."

"What are you waiting for?" The captain shouted, roaring with pain as he yanked the blade Queen Naz stabbed him with from his arm.

Sweat once again blanketed Timur's brow, his hands shaking as his perplexed heart cried out for him to wait. What if he was making a grave mistake in trusting the captain? What if Adel's death was a part of the plan all along?

Shaking his head, he pushed these thoughts from his mind. Whatever the plan, the woman before him needed to die. The sight of her hand thrusting the arrow into Adel's rib case urged his decision.

With one final breath, he let go of the string. The arrow pierced her beating chest and her eyes widened. Her fingers trembled as they wrapped around the arrow. Confusion filled her eyes as they iced over. He watched as her body fell limp at his feet.

"Good work." The captain's voice neared.

He looked grimly down at the old man, still cradling his shoulder.

"And now once we've capture the sultan we will be able to rebuild the empire. Begin a new dawn for the Ubir. You will be involved, of course." Captain Yusuf smiled as if any of these things would please him.

Dark creases lined Timur's forehead, still damp with sweat.

"I've only just killed the queen," Timur said. "And now you speak of capturing an innocent man? Haven't enough innocent people fallen at your hand?"

The captain chuckled "If you're speaking of Adel, I can assure you he was no innocent."

"Don't you dare speak his name," Timur snarled.

"Adel knew the risk, the price this mission could require—"

"He knew what you told him! What you told us," Timur's fangs punctured through his gums, anger soaring through his veins. "Adel wasn't supposed to be in the courtyard."

"Adel followed my orders exactly," the captain's voice darkened. "And so will you."

"No," Timur shook his head, backing away. "I've taken out the queen. I've completed my obligation to you."

"You could have a seat at the Imperial Council," the captain offered. "Think of the change we could make together! Timur!"

He turned towards the courtyard's exit, leaving the desperate captain behind him.

"You will regret this!" Yusuf bellowed, but only the rising sun could hear his empty threat.

***

The next morning had come too quickly for Emel, bringing with it Gelin Alma. The time had come for the groom's family and guests to fetch her, the evidence of their arrival shaking the walls. The beat of their drums and cheerful cries grew louder as Emel said her final goodbyes to her family.

Covered from head to toe, she pulled at the hot fabric as each one of her family members embraced her.

"Remember, this is an honor," her mother whispered in her ear. Funda's disapproving look warning her to stop fidgeting. "And if you try to run again, well, your father will be less forgiving."

Emel grimaced, stilling her antsiness. She didn't want to believe that this would be her life. She had so much more she wanted to do, to see and experience. And would she ever see Timur again? What if something happened to him after confronting his friend? The thought occurred to her in a dream and it caused her to panic. Perhaps he was injured or worse, killed. She shuddered at the thought of this. If only her plan to escape had worked. She had tied fabric together and had reached the row of silk trees, but her mother was there. Waiting for her. How had she known?

"Farewell, sister." Sidika smiled with every attempt at being polite, but the sentiment never reached her eyes.

"Goodbye," Emel whispered, forcing the thought that her sister might've had a hand in it as far down as she could.

Once her last goodbyes were through, a red belt was tied around her waist before being quickly ushered out the front door.

"Are you ready?" Manula asked, leading her from the home.

Emel's heart ached as she breathed in the sweet honey of the silk trees that perfumed the breeze for the last time. She scanned the many faces that greeted them as they emerged into the courtyard.

"No," she finally replied. But no one cared.

Tears stung as she stepped out into the courtyard towards the horse that was offered to her. A four-posted canopy was mounted to the horse's back, the silk fabric fluttering in the hot breeze.

Pipes blared and voices cheered as she mounted, the silk walls of the canopy pulled closed so that only her silhouette could be seen.

Her heart leapt as she saw the janissaries at the front of the procession, clad in their ceremonial garb. She scanned each soldier for Timur's curly, black hair, a glimpse of his broad shoulders or even his deep sorrel eyes. But no matter how much she willed him to be among them, he was nowhere to be found. Her hope sank as the horse was slowly led, by four men, away from her home.

She took in the last glimpses of the only place she'd ever known. The sight of her father, uncles, and cousins marching behind her reminded her of the life she was leaving behind. But she didn't have a choice, did she?

As the crowd moved through busy streets many stopped to watch the celebration. Men danced about in front of her carriage, strangers hollered and cheered. Seeing all the happiness that surrounded her couldn't lighten her spirits. It should've been a joyful day. A day of adventure spent with Timur as they fled for a new life. Instead, she was on her way to a life of emptiness.

***

Timur sprinted down the stone path towards the nishanji's home, the rising sun warning he was too late. Throwing care to the wind, he urged his Ubirdi muscles forward. Each step brought him closer to where his heart would be. As he raced along the infinite rows of adobe and wood homes, Emel's eyes were all he saw. Luscious blue irises with golden tendrils that danced like stars. To be in her presence again was the only cure he needed. The thirst for blood raged its evil head, threatening to rip him apart. If only he could be with Emel again, he would once again be whole. He would embrace her, allow the calming waters of her very soul to wash away the darkness that threatened his entirety. And he would care for her in a way no one else could. He would protect her with every fiber of his being.

"Wait!" He called after a maid who was closing the front gate of Emel's home.

The petite woman glanced suspiciously at him, threatening to slam the door in his face. He recognized the locket she wore at her neck and realized it was Manula.

"Emel, is she here?" He huffed, surprised at being so out of breath.

Manula shook her head. "They've just taken her. Why do you ask?"

"Taken her?" His eyebrows furrowed, not understanding.

"Gelin Alma." Manula looked at him as though he should've known. "She's on her way to the chief judge's home. You didn't know she was arranged to marry Hamid? The judge's son?"

"No." He then realized where he'd heard that name and suddenly it all made sense. "You said they went this way?"

He pointed down the narrow road leading past the home. Manula began to nod, but then her eyes widened as if she had just recognized him.

"You're the solak from the street," Manula gasped.

"Yes, I am, but I'm very much in a hurry. Thank you!" He called before dashing off, determination filling his every bone.

The beating of drums met his ear and he pushed himself faster. A crowd was building and he forged his way through.

"STOP!" He shouted, his eyes locked on the steed carrying the only person that truly mattered to him.

The horse halted, the four men leading the animal attempted to prod it along but there was no use. His power was too strong.

The wind blew past Timur as he raced faster than humanly possible. He was a blur to the crowd, flying towards the canopy. Reaching his target, he pulled the drapes open.

"Timur?" The melody of Emel's voice asked from behind a thick veil.

Pulling the thick cloth from her head, time stopped as she washed over him like waves.

"I thought you'd never come," she said, her eyes tearing at the sight of him.

"Nothing in the world could stop me from returning to you," he whispered, taking her hand in his. "Come, we've no time."

"Unhand her!" A dull voice ordered as a fist pulled him from the canopy.

The Ubir who stood before Timur was none other than Emel's father, his narrow eyes flashing crimson. Shouts alerted him to the crowd that surrounded them.

"You will leave or this shall be your last mistake." Timur respected the calm nature of the nishanji, but there was no way he would be leaving without Emel.

Hasan-Ali extended his Ubirdi claws, as if he had forgotten they were surrounded by humans. Screams echoed in the streets as those nearby fled.

"You would dare to expose what you are?" Timur stood his ground.

"I would dare to keep my daughter from the likes of you." Hasan-Ali scowled.

"From me?" He raised an eyebrow. "Wasn't it you who accepted private meetings with Chief Judge Halil? Who promised his own daughter to the judge's son in exchange for a title?"

"That is none of your concern," Hasan-Ali replied, flatly

"But it is my concern that the grand vizier was murdered and it's not *my* hands that are bloody."

Hasan-Ali lunged at Timur, smashing him to the ground. "The only blood I'll have on my hands is yours."

The nishanji lifted his fist, preparing to smash it into his face.

"NO!" He heard Emel shriek from under the canopy, struggling to dismount.

Timur grabbed Hasan-Ali's fist just in time, shoving him so hard the old man flew into the air, crashing against the adobe wall of the nearby building.

"You had the chief judge kill the grand vizier," Timur spat, rising up from the ground. "And you would have had me take the fall for it!"

Hasan-Ali coughed as he pulled himself up, dusting off his robe.

"It was merely a suggestion, how could I know the chief judge would actually do it." The nishanji chuckled as if a man's death was some kind of joke.

Timur growled, his rage threatening to take hold.

"You may be strong," Hasan-Ali shrugged. "But my daughter is coming with me."

Emel's feet barely reached the ground when Hasan-Ali suddenly grabbed her, yanking her away from Timur.

"No, let me *go*!" She wailed, pushing against him.

"Silence," Hasan-Ali ordered, slapping Emel across the cheek causing her to fall to her knees.

Timur couldn't hold the anger in anymore and sprang forward, pinning Hasan-Ali against the wall. The mud and stone threatened to cave from the force of it. Heat rose from every muscle in Timur's body as rage filled him. Gripping Hasan-Ali's neck, he lifted him up off of his feet. The nishanji's clawed arms lashed out, but he was no match for Timur.

"Wait!" Emel's desperate voice cried. Her hand rested on his arm and he looked at her.

A pink and purple bruise left on her injured cheek made him tighten his grip on the despicable man.

"Don't do it," she pleaded, worry creasing her brow. "Don't give in to the beast. You're not like my father."

He glanced back at Hasan-Ali, his fearful eyes begging for his life. The old man didn't deserve Emel's mercy. But then, neither did he.

Without another word, he dropped his hold on the nishanji, letting him fall to the ground.

"Let's go," Emel said, taking Timur's hand.

Hasan-Ali coughed bitterly, attempting to pull himself in protest. Timur desperately wanted to punish the man before him, but the warmth of Emel's hand stopped him.

Before the nishanji could stop him, he wrapped his arm about Emel's waist and launched them into the air. The rushing wind filled his ears as he maneuvered his body like a seagull heading for the bay.

The music of Emel's delighted screams reached his ear and he glanced down at her, resting easily in his arms. He was sure he'd never get used to being in the presence of someone as perfect as her. They landed gently on the beach they'd met at just the other day, the cliff wall protecting them from the wind. Setting her gently on her feet, he grasped her hands in his.

"Are you okay?"

"With you? I've never been better." She flashed him a dazzling smile that crinkled her eyelids, sending his heart soaring.

"Where to now?"

"To Chios, of course," she said gleefully, her breath sending chills down his arms.

She wrapped her hands around his neck, her longing eyes searching his and for a moment everything around him vanished. Lowering his gaze, his lips gently pulled hers into an embrace filled with love. A love he never knew existed, but one he now could not live without.

THE END.

Epilogue

The crimson eyes of Queen Naz flew open as her lungs filled with air. Her chest heaved as a loud gasp escaped her lips.

Sitting up, her back was as straight as a board. She looked down at the dried blood surrounding the arrow and pulled it from her chest, as if it were a splinter.

"Well, now I know where my son's loyalty lies," she hissed.

Pulling herself up, the gray signs of decay softened as her energy returned.

"Bayar, it's time to wake up now" she smiled, letting her neck lean towards either side as her strained muscles cracked into place.

Gliding towards the eunuch's side, she quickly removed the arrow from his heart.

"Bayar." She leaned in, her lips trailing his ear. "Are you up?"

The man's tall body twitched, a shudder escaping his lips as life returned to him.

"H-how?" Bayar stuttered, his eyes wide with shock once he was able to speak. "How am I—?"

"Alive?" Gazing down upon the kizlar chief, a devilish grin spread upon her face. "What kind of queen would I be without a few tricks up my sleeve?

"You are a magnificent queen," Bayar chuckled in delight, spitting old blood from his lip.

"Indeed," she smiled. "Now come, let's go find the captain before he makes another error in judgment."

The kizlar chief rose, towering above the queen. Motioning for him to follow her, she slunk towards the hallway leading deep within the palace. She could smell the captain's essence growing stronger. Whatever they'd drenched themselves in the night before must've been wearing off.

The aroma grew stronger as they moved towards the sultan's open door. A struggle echoed from within the room, the sun beaming in from the tinted glass ceilings.

"Yusuf, sweetie?" She cooed, strolling into the open bedchamber.

On a white, silken bed the body of the sultan lay, his empty gaze witnessing their arrival. Blood seeped from his neck, the stain beneath him indicating he hadn't died that long ago. Captain Yusuf stood by the bedside, hunched over the body. Looking up, his lips covered in blood, the captain flushed white when he saw Queen Naz and Bayar.

"Allah, Allah!" Yusuf gasped, moving from the bed. "You're supposed to be dead!"

"And who do I have to thank for that?" She raised an eyebrow.

The captain shook vigorously as he stared into the eyes of the queen. Fear creased his brow as she neared.

"But the bow...," he trailed, panic setting in. "I saw it plunge into your heart. It was drenched in Timur's blood! He is your son, was your son..."

"Honestly, Yusuf." She peered down at the stocky man, failing in his attempts at shrinking away from her. "Who do you think spread that rumor in the first place?"

Before the captain could utter another word, Queen Naz plunged her fangs into his neck, sucking him dry.

More Transitioned Universe Books

A SUPERNATURAL ACADEMY TRILOGY

Tompkin's School: For The Extraordinarily Talented
Tompkin's School: For The Dearly Departed
Tompkin's School: For The Resurrected

GASLAMP FANTASY & DETECTIVE MYSTERY

The Unforgivable Act
The Detective's Nightmare
The Yuletide Killer

Grab a copy from your favorite bookstore!

www.goodreads.com/tabislick

Glossary

Abzar İyesi - A creature which acts as a guardian spirit of the courtyard or front garden of the home. It can take the shape of any animal. (See Bibliography [17]).

Agha - The general officer of the janissaries. (See Bibliography [1, 4]).

Allah'a şükür - Thank God.

Bezesten - An enclosed marketplace much like a mosque. (See Bibliography [1]).

Constantinople - Present day Istanbul. Constantinople was the official name of Istanbul until the mid 20th century. (See Bibliography [3]).

Divan-ı Hümâyûn - The Imperial Council. (See Bibliography [15]).

Eid al-Fitr - A three day long holiday after the fast. (See Bibliography [1]).

Erguvan Tree (a.k.a. "Judas tree") - A bright purple flowering tree that blooms in the spring and native to Turkey. (See Bibliography [7]

Eunuch - Certain slaves were castrated to become eunuchs. Only black eunuchs were allowed inside the Harem. Some eunuchs retained sexual abilities and desires. If this was discovered they would be killed. (See Bibliography [1, 5]).

Franks - Anyone who is not Turkish. (See Bibliography [1]).

Friday Selamlik - Friday Prayer. Sultans would ride out surrounded by their guards on their way to the Imperial mosque. (See Bibliography [12, 15]).

Gelin Alma - To fetch the bride on the wedding day. (See Bibliography [15]).

Görücülük - The act of examining a woman as a potential bride. This is done by a woman, usually by the mother with sons of marriageable age. (See Bibliography [10, 15]).

Helva (a.k.a. "Halva" or "Çövenç") - A dessert commonly sold on the streets in Constantinople during the 17th century. Legend has it that Çövenç is the source of strength and vitality symbolizing the transition from this universe after death. (See Bibliography [1, 14, 17]).

Hortlak - Turkish equivalent to a zombie. (See Bibliography [17]).

Hünnap - Also known as Jujube, this fruit grows from a flowering tree. The fruit is reddish-brown and its proportion is similar to an olive. (See Bibliography [14]).

Iftar - The meal eaten after sundown during Ramadan. (See Bibliography [14, 15]).

Janissary - A soldier in the Turkish army. (See Bibliography [1, 4, 8]).

Kına Gecesi - A Henna party held on the last night the bride spends in her family's home. Women of both families attend. (See Bibliography [15]).

Kingfisher - A small bird native to Turkey with blue and golden brown feathers. (See Bibliography [11]).

Kiraz - Cherries. The sultan's important guests and visiting ambassadors were often served a feast including cherry pudding and sherbet. (See Bibliography [14]).

Kizi - Daughter. Before surnames were implemented, names consisted only of the father's name followed by 'kizi' plus the daughter's name. (See Bibliography [13]).

Kizlar Chief (or "Kilzaragasi") - Chief of the girls. This position was held by a black eunuch in charge of the Harem. The Kizlaragasi often had political power. "Agasi" is the equivalent to Chief which is used in this story for simplicity. (See Bibliography [1, 5]).

Köçek - Male dancers known to wear skirts and try to act like girls through dances. They performed in public, unlike the female dancers who only performed in front of other women. (See Bibliography [1, 15]).

Leventis - Naval soldiers that caused a lot of trouble for Constantinople. The three curses were considered "pestilence, fires, and the leventis". (See Bibliography [1]).

Mangala - A game played with seashells and was often enjoyed by Turkish women during the 17th century. (See Bibliography [1]).

Mech - A short sword. (See Bibliography [15]).

Medlar (a.k.a. "Musmula") - A brown fruit that grows on a short tree. (See Bibliography [14]).

Nishanji - Chancellor of the records. This position was in charge of sealing all of the Sultan's documents. (See Bibliography [4]).

Oglu - Son. Before surnames were implemented, names consisted only of the father's name followed by 'oglu' plus the son's name. (See Bibliography [13]).

Ottoman lake - The Black Sea was often regarded as the Ottoman lake between the 15th and 17th centuries. (See Bibliography [3]).

Ramadan - A religious fast practiced each year by Islam that lasts for thirties days. (See Bibliography [1, 10, 15]).

Simit - A round, Turkish bread usually made with sesame seeds or sunflower seeds. (See Bibliography [14]).

Sofa - A large room much like the living rooms today, positioned at the outer wall of the home. (See Bibliography [16]).

Solak - A left handed bowman who served as the Sultan's personal guard. (See Bibliography [1, 9]).

Salatu-l-Fajr - Early morning prayer. (See Bibliography [10]).

Söz Kesimi - A promise or agreement to marriage. (See Bibliography [15]).

Tandir - A low table with a burner underneath to provide warmth. It is covered with an ornate cover that reaches the floor and surrounded by couches. (See Bibliography [1]).

Tutku flower - Passion flower herb. In this story it is used to suppress the Ubir's thirst for blood. It tastes of grass with notes of berry.

Valide Sultan - The title of "mother sultan" was given to the deceased sultan's chief escort if her son became the sultan. The valide sultan had a lot of power over the harem as well as in political affairs. (See Bibliography [1, 9, 10, 15]).

Ubir (or "Ubirdi") - A vampire in Turkish mythology. According to their legend, Ubirdi people look for food at night and, if they cannot find blood to drink, will turn into flames. (See Bibliography [2, 6, 17]).

Yasmak - Turkish covering made of silk. One piece of the cloth was worn to cover the head and upper forehead, the second piece of cloth covered the mouth and nose. (See Bibliography [1, 10]).

Bibliography

[1] *An Album of the Wardrobe of The Ottomans With Illustrations by The Tulip-Era Artist Van Mour / Lale Devri Ressami Van Mour"un Cizimleriyle Osmanlilar Kiyafet Albumu.* Istanbul: Istanbul Metropolitan Municipality Kulur A.S., 1714 (2013).

[2] Evliya Çelebi. *Seyahatname vol. 7.* Edited by Seyit Ali Kahraman, Yücel Dağlı, and Robert Dankoff. Istanbul: Yapı Kredi Yayınları, 2003.

[3] Finkel, Caroline. *Osman's Dream: The History of the Ottoman Empire.* Basic Books, 2007.

[4] Imber, Colin. *The Ottoman Empire 1300-1650: The Structure of Power.* New York: Palgrace Macmillan, 2009.

[5] Juune, George. *Black Eunuchs of the Ottoman Empire.* London: I.B. Tauris & Co. Ltd, 2016.

[6] Kırgi, Salim Fikret. *An Early Modern Horror Story.* Central European university History Department, 2017.

[7] Kayahan, Ayşe Betül. *Istanbul's Purple Grace.* Daily Sabah, 2014.

[8] Lewis, Bernard. *Istanbul and the Civilization of the Ottoman Empire.* Norman: University of Oklahoma Press, 1963.

[9] Ozgen, Korkut. *TheOttomans.org.* LuckyEye Limited, 2002.

[10] Sansal, Burak H. *AllAboutTurkey.com.* All About Turkey, 2017.

[11] Sawe, Benjamin Elisha. *Native Birds of Turkey.* WorldAtlas.com, 2018.

[12] Taglia, Steano. *Intellectuals and Reform in the Ottoman Empire*. London: Routledge, 2015.

[13] "The Origin of Current Greek and Turkish Surnames." *Pontosworld.com*. PontosWorld, 2018.

[14] *TurkishCuisine.org*. Turkish Cultural Foundation, 2018.

[15] *TurkishCulture.org*. Turkish Cultural Foundation, 2018

[16] "Turkish Houses." *Kulturturizm.gov.tr*. Ministry of Culture and Tourism, 2018.

[17] *Türk Söylence Sözlüğü*. Deniz Karakurt, 2011.

Acknowledgements

I have to give a shout out to my wonderful sidekick, Dexter, who put up with all of my crazy music for days on end while writing this story. This German Shepherd and Rhodesian Ridgeback didn't complain once (although I did occasionally receive a couple of sad puppy dog eyes when I wouldn't share my snacks. I usually caved and shared).

Thanks to my editor, Sarah, for challenging my writing and pushing me to improve. I've learned so much and believe my story is better for it. When I had to have surgery, she totally worked with my schedule and I sincerely appreciate her understanding. She is straightforward and to the point with her editing and will often give you suggestions, which I thought was amazing! She even helped brainstorm ideas when I hit writer's block. I cannot rave enough about my editor.

I would also like to thank all my friends who inspired and encouraged me to write this story. You know I was nervous about taking on this project, but each one of you instilled a confidence in me to push forward and I'm sincerely grateful for your friendship.

To all who helped me in shaping this story (you know who you are) I thank you from the bottom of my heart.

About the Author

TABI SLICK is an award-winning author of paranormal and historical fantasy. Her younger years were spent living in the countryside of Oklahoma until she started her college studies in Puerto Rico. After several years abroad, she finally settled down in the Dallas-Fort Worth area of Texas.

With a background in Linguistics, she's often found either researching or with her nose stuck in a book. She's not only the wife of a systems engineer, and mother to a beautiful German Shepherd and Rhodesian Ridgeback pup, but she's also a blogger and book ninja.

Learn more about Tabi and her books at:
www.TabiSlick.com

Connect with the Author

Follow on Social Media:
www.Facebook.com/TabiSlick
www.twitter.com/TabiSlick
www.Instagram.com/TabiSlick

Monthly Bookish Digest:
http://newsletter.tabislick.com/subscribe

Leave a review for Timur's Escape by visiting:

www.goodreads.com/book/show/43299999-timur-s-escape

www.ingramcontent.com/pod-product-compliance
Lightning Source LLC
Chambersburg PA
CBHW021946290426
44108CB00012B/978